From the author of the best
selling books "Single Again"
and "Married Again" comes a
new book directed to widows: GEORGE B. BLAKE

I0003271

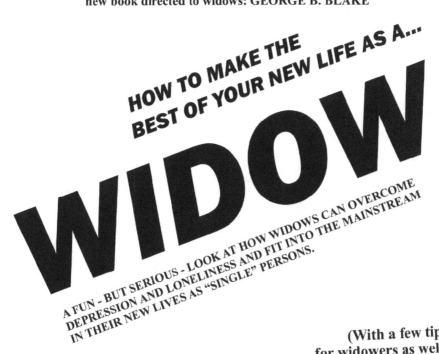

HOW TO MAKE THE BEST OF YOUR NEW LIFE AS A...
WIDOW

A FUN - BUT SERIOUS - LOOK AT HOW WIDOWS CAN OVERCOME DEPRESSION AND LONELINESS AND FIT INTO THE MAINSTREAM IN THEIR NEW LIVES AS "SINGLE" PERSONS.

(With a few tips
for widowers as well)

Read what widowed women say sparked their lives in
today's "single" world.

"Singles" now outnumber marrieds in the USA for the first time
in history. As a widow, you are now part of this new majority.
This book will help you adjust to your new life after experiencing
the most awful tragedy imaginable: the passing of a loved one.

outskirtspress
DENVER, COLORADO

The opinions expressed in this manuscript are solely the opinions of the author and do not represent the opinions or thoughts of the publisher. The author has represented and warranted full ownership and/or legal right to publish all the materials in this book.

Widow
How to Make the Best of Your New Life as a...
All Rights Reserved.
Copyright © 2014 George B. Blake
v3.0

Cover Photo © 2014 George B. Blake. All rights reserved - used with permission.

This book may not be reproduced, transmitted, or stored in whole or in part by any means, including graphic, electronic, or mechanical without the express written consent of the publisher except in the case of brief quotations embodied in critical articles and reviews.

Outskirts Press, Inc.
http://www.outskirtspress.com

ISBN: 978-1-4787-3959-3

Library of Congress Control Number: 2014912071

Outskirts Press and the "OP" logo are trademarks belonging to Outskirts Press, Inc.

PRINTED IN THE UNITED STATES OF AMERICA

THANKS TO . . .

the widows who took the time and effort
to contribute their experiences and ideas
for the well-being of all single persons.

THANKS A BUNCH!

Contents

Introduction

Welcome to my new book devoted to widows (and in some instances widowers as well). I must admit that I devote more attention to widows because they outnumber widowers (and single men in general) by such a large margin...in many areas as much as ten to one. That can force lonely widows to being even lonelier when it comes to social interaction...unless they pay attention to the many tips found in this book, and which ones fit their individual personalties. First, let me list my credentials for those widows who ask "who the hell is he?" Here are the facts: I have spent about half of my life organizing events where singles can meet other singles (Attention widows: you are now a single person, so get used to it!) I wrote a syndicated "singles" newspaper column for 14 years. I organized and promoted over 1,400 singles events (tennis, golf, bridge, cocktail parties, dances, cruises, happy hours, etc., attended by over 450,000 single people. The very few times that there was a small admission charge, 100% of the proceeds went to a very needy local charity.

I also participated in 159 talk shows around the USA on radio and TV call-in programs so I have had plenty of nationwide experience talking with lonely widows and answering their mail. I also wrote five books about singles (I use some material in this book from my big seller "Single Again: Dating And Meeting New Friends The Second Time Around", and another of my popular books "Married Again: Making The Right Decision The Next Time")

Though my main goal is to help widows and newly divorced singles overcome loneliness, I have incidentally caused hundreds of singles to meet a new soul-mate and get re-married. (And I might add, successfully).

You'll see as you read along that I always emphasize the "positive" side of life, with lots of humor thrown in. It's the only way to go! So if you are a widow (or widower) and you are trying to recover from the greatest loss a person can ever have - the passing of a loved one - I hope you'll like my feeble attempt to bring back some joy into your life! But the next step belongs to you!

This book offers case histories and success (or failure) stories about problems and OPPORTUNITIES that inure to "second-time" singles in their everyday social lives. I've changed names and places, so no one can accuse me of spilling the beans on their secret lives; other than that, all the stories and events are true. While I do give a few suggestions and recommendations, they are based on what is really happening in the singles world, rather than on what people *wish* were happening or might *think* is happening. You'll see that I don't pull any punches and that I tell it like it is, so put on your thick skin, and jump right in.

To make the book livelier, I have interspersed stories and commentary with letters from some of the thousands of people who have written my newspaper column about their experiences as second-time singles.

With 100 million singles already in the market and an additional 5 million people joining the singles scene each year, there certainly should be a lot of people out there who will find this book a helpful shortcut to "jumpstart" the rest of their lives. At least I hope so.

So I wrote this book motivated by a sense of wanting to help newly single people and widows get off on the right foot and giving long-time singles some new ammunition to help improve their lifestyles.

And I might add that the thought of 100 million $ingle$ buying this book also crossed my mind.

George B. Blake

Chapter One

WIDOW'S SPEAK

I have been fortunate to have received thousands of letters and e-mails from widows outlining their plight in their suddenly new life, and what they did to make their life right again. Here are a few of these letters:

From A Widow's View

Dear George:

. . . "Where am I?" . . . "What am I doing here, anyway?" . . . "This is all just a hideous nightmare, right? . . . ***Wrong!!*** *These are just a few of the things that can go through a widow's mind, especially once the initial "shock" has started to wear off and reality sets in: I am truly alone, again.*

"O.K., so you've managed to survive the aftermath of it all: relatives have returned home, friends have gone on their merry way and here you are, on your own, . . . but, what do I do now? Is it alright to go to a restaurant alone? But, more importantly, do I want to go alone?!!

"Being suddenly "tossed" out into the single world after being happily married for a number of years can be very difficult, challenging, and, at times, profoundly overwhelming. But one thing I have learned as hard as it is, unless you take that first step and move forward, no one is going to do it for you! You and you alone are in control of your life.

"So, where do you start? Having moved only two months after my husband passed away just added to my complex situation. I knew no one and no one knew me. That can certainly make things rather

difficult . . . but situations are truly what you make it. So, after a number of months of "hibernating", I decided it was time for me to move on. I "took the plunge" and decided to try kayaking . . . and that "first step" forward literally changed my life! I gained a new confidence I never knew I had, and I have met some wonderful people and gone on numerous other "paddles" since then.

"Going to the restaurant for the first time **alone** was another major challenge for me. I would have never considered doing something like that in the past . . . but, this was no longer the past! Once you get by that "first time" syndrome, however, it **does** get easier, believe me. And, then, there are the singles functions and "bar/lounge scene" . . . whew, talk about apprehension!! I felt I really had to swallow hard to get by this one . . . but, you know what?? I did it and I survived!! (...thanks to encouragement from your "singles" column.) And, yes, it does open up a whole new world for you . . . you just need to hold your head high, open your eyes, and be willing to embrace those opportunities that are out there waiting for you."

Here's another letter from a lovely widow:

Dear George:

"When I learned that you were writing a new book directed to widows, I thought you might like to read about my experiences.

"My husband and I were happily married for 29 years. We were both friends and lovers. We went everywhere together and thoroughly enjoyed each other's company. When he passed away unexpectedly, I suddenly felt alone, depressed and unsure of myself. I was still working and that saved my life. After several months of feeling sorry for myself, I realized that I didn't like my new life as a lonely loner. So after work and on weekends, I attended every event I could: church, sports events, horse shows, pet shows, charities, shopping sales, business meetings, business trips...everything to keep my mind busy. My relatives treated me as a mature adult, not *as a weepy widow, and that helped. I learned to dine out and travel by myself. I kept busy in public venues, not lonely ones. I made a rule that I don't babysit with my grandkids unless its an emergency.*

"And now since I only have one mouth to feed, I feel I can splurge a little and move on with my life. I bought new living room and family room furniture and lots of clothes to fill my suddenly vacant closets. Being a woman, this helped a lot. I figured - though I still love and miss my husband greatly - that I've turned a "negative" into a "positive". It's the only way to go.

"I know he is up there smiling at me, saying his usual expression. .. "you go girl!"."

How about this letter that shows a real success story:

Dear George:

"WIDOW! What a cruel word that can be, even if you think you've done everything you could to prepare yourself. When my husband of 25 years went into a nursing home with a terminal illness, I thought I was doing exactly that. After two years in the nursing home, I was almost used to living alone. When the end came, I was going to be just fine I thought. WRONG!

"When everything quieted down after the funeral, I'd wake up in the morning and realize...I'M ALONE! No more spending every day with him at the nursing home. How was I going to live without him? And also, what was I going to do to fill my lonely days.

"I guess the thing that topped all this off and almost left me in a state of shock was the first time I had to fill out a form that asked for marital status. Of course, I had to check WIDOW. WIDOW? Who me? I am, aren't I. I don't want to be. It can't be real. But unfortunately it was.

"So although I had thought myself preparing for this for two years, nothing prepares you for being a widow. My advice to new widows is to do what I am now doing: continue the activities in which

you've always been involved. I'd even go alone to our favorite bar/ restaurant where we felt comfortable because we had been regulars there before his illness advanced. The friends I had and the ones I have made since becoming a widow, along with my church activities, have been my salvation.

"I often tell other new widows to just get out there and make another life for yourself. You will find that you can enjoy life again. You might even be fortunate enough to meet a nice man whose company you enjoy, just as I have. Life goes on and you need to go along with it."

The tone of most of the letters I received is that widows need to be upbeat and positive, and keep their eyes wide open for new opportunities to do new things. Opportunities are just around the corner (except for this widower's letter who jumped-in with both eyes SHUT!)

Dear George:

"My wife passed away 2 years ago after 27 years of marriage. I was so lonely for someone to talk to every night that before I realized it, I had remarried. And I might add that I remarried without really knowing much about my new partner. Now that we have lived together for about a year, we realize too late that we don't have anything in common, and, unfortunately, we get on each other's nerves.

"We are parting gracefully, but everything is in such turmoil that I wish I had known from the start to become acquainted with more single women so that I could have made a more rational decision. Maybe if you print this letter, other widowers will be warned not to jump into the first dating situation that presents itself but to look around and date a number of women to be sure of making the right decision. In my haste to find another "friend" like I had in my original marriage, I only found trouble. I was better off being lonely."

Unfortunately, I know a number of widowers who suffered this same sad experience. And the thing that hurts the most is that these guys are really good people who would be loyal husbands and great companions to a new wife. But they all selected the first gal and jumped into a hasty marriage or relationship.

Follow the advice of this letter writer, men, and get to know several great women before you settle on the best one.

Chapter Two

WHAT'S AHEAD FOR YOU AS A SINGLE PERSON!

(You'll notice that I gradually drop the title of "Widow"!)

I know that by the time you read and digest the ideas in this book, you will still respect the memory of your departed loved ones even more than today; and you'll begin to realize that they want you to move on with your life without them because they want their memory to continue to be that of a caring person who always wants the best for you.

Now let's look at your new exciting life as a single person.

I'm sure some readers are thinking "exciting"? What's so exciting about not having a mate or companion around all the time? But really, that's the exciting part of it. As you seek a new mate/companion, you'll see that a whole new world will open before you...a world of meeting a variety of interesting people, going to a variety of interesting places, and doing a variety of interesting things. You'll go to places and do things that you probably didn't get a chance to do in your marriage, or didn't even know existed. That's the "excitement" of "single" life. And now that single adults in the USA outnumber married adults for the first time in history, you now are a member of a "majority." That must make you even more excited.

One thing you must resolve in your own mind is to agree to go forth *right now* and begin to follow the ideas and suggestions in this book. Remember! We're not getting any younger; and, unlike good bourbon, we don't necessarily get better with age either.

That's why I get impatient with single people who are slow to

---

change and adapt to the new single life in which they find themselves. That's why I don't beat around the bush but get right to the heart of the situation. I'm brutally honest, and this honesty and impatience can sometimes be misconstrued as male chauvinism. But nothing is farther from the truth.

There are many millions more adult single women than adult single men, and it has been my experience that the majority of widows are much slower than widowers to accept the fact that they are now single again. Things can be very different for them---and sometimes very difficult for them—the second time around, and I want to help them get through the difficult periods. I get impatient and antsy at the slow pace of some of these people to accept their new status, and it may show from time to time. Please bear with me. Maybe I need to pray for patience:

LORD, GIVE ME PATIENCE!
BUT I WANT IT *RIGHT NOW*!

Some people's problems are due to their own personalties, and no one can help them except themselves. People who are rude, pushy, macho, negative, conceited, battle axes, etc., etc., can only change by changing their outlooks on life. They'll recognize their personality traits—or shortcomings—as they read on, and I hope they will want to modify them so that they'll better fit into today's singles society.

Here's what happened to a reader who followed my suggestions:

Dear George:

"I am a 44 year-old attractive female. I thought I would look and feel "cheap" if I went to a singles party or dance, and I was fiercely determined never to stoop so low as to go to one. But, finally, my loneliness and the persistence of your urgings in your newspaper column induced me to go to a singles activity one evening. It took all the courage I could muster.

"As it turned out, no one thought I was "cheap," and in fact, hardly anyone even noticed me. I thought I would stand out in the crowd as a newcomer (or worse, a brazen man-hunter) and that everyone would stare. But like everything else, it too was a figment of my imagination. No one treated me rudely or with any disrespect. I was left free to do what I wanted and to talk to whomever I pleased, with no hassles.

"I hate to admit it, but I found the singles atmosphere less intimidating than all the parties I attended with my husband. Thanks to you, George, I'm getting my act together and getting out again. Spread the word to other women who are wasting their time alone. God bless you!"

To people like this reader, the singles scene was thought of as being dreadful and foreboding until they decided to check it out for themselves. And that's the best advice I can give you. Don't rely on rumors. Don't let "marrieds" tell you what's going on in the singles world. And for goodness sake, don't listen to all the bunk that is dished out by the media about the poor plight of single people. Check out the local singles scene on your own. See for yourself what really goes on. In the *vast majority* of cases, you'll be pleasantly surprised.

Many who took my suggestions have found the OPPORTUNITY to enjoy a really fulfilling life as a single man or woman once again. They gave themselves a second chance, so to speak, to restart their lives. They attacked this new challenge with vigor and enthusiasm. They're my kind of people.

The singles scene need not be scary or dreadful any more than being married should be. And just as it's true that all marriages and all married people aren't good or happy, so too all single people and all single events aren't 100 percent good. You are going to run into a few bad apples whatever your lifestyle. So when you do encounter a bad one, don't get discouraged. *It's the exception.* Move on!

The singles scene has been unfairly portrayed by various individuals as a low-class, desperate way of life. That's rubbish!

These naysayers seem to pick out one or two instances of singles with problems and then milk them to death for years on end until we come to believe that these problems coexist with single life. It's a lot of baloney. I can think of a lot more "marrieds" with problems, and so can you! So let's all be "positive."

A major problem with the singles scene is the lopsided ratio of single women to single men, which I mentioned earlier. Except for five sparsely populated states in the USA, single women outnumber single men in every state in the union (and most Canadian provinces) by wide margins. In some metropolitan markets, adult single women outnumber their male counterparts by as much as ten to one! And that's where you'll find what I call the "singles jungle": women fighting for dates; women fighting for affection; women fighting for male attention. And this problem begets another problem: Some single men who suddenly realize they are "in demand" tend to become overconfident, overbearing and downright conceited and obnoxious, (even though some of them, if the ratios were reversed, probably couldn't get a date in a hundred years, even with a "fistful of fifties").

I describe these and many other "inhabitants: of the "singles scene" on the succeeding pages. And guess what? Someplace in this book you are likely to find a description of *yourself*. Whether or not you like this description and whether or not you want to change what you see remains your decision. But most of you ARE included in this book.

Isn't it nice being a celebrity?

You've Got To Be Creative!

In the singles world, it's survival of the "fittest," and often the fittest are those who are the most creative. You'll get a lot of creative ideas as you read on, but I just had to highlight this one woman from an Illinois suburb. She came up with a very creative idea on how to meet successful bachelors, and she met a bunch of them!

Her brother happened to own a classic 1962 sports car, which he let her "borrow" for her creative experiment. She placed a classified ad in the "Classic Cars For Sale" section in her local newspaper. She listed her brother's classic car for sale to the best offer and described it generously. She received 51 calls to her ad, and as she suspected, most just happened to be successful single men...the kind who had sufficient disposable income to be able to afford a classic such as this. Of course, they all wanted to look at the car, and as they inspected it, she inspected them. It was a great conversation starter, and seven of the men ended up asking her for a date.

And, as she knew would be the case, none of them made an "acceptable" offer for her brother's car (which he didn't want to sell anyway). But she got a lot of "mileage" from it without ever taking it out of the driveway. If you want to meet the cream of the singles crop, a little creativity goes a long way.

A Look At Today's Singles

You might say that the appropriate motto for modern-day singles is "do your own thing" as long as you don't hurt another person or yourself. And while we all must respect a person's upbringing, religious beliefs, and social or familial mores, I think Victorian customs from that long ago era should be tossed in the ash can if you are going to make it as a second-time single.

Dear George:

"My girlfriend calls men on the telephone all the time. As a lady, I think it's tacky and pushy, and I told her so. Maybe you can correct her."

Maybe instead I should try to correct YOU! What law— religious social, or moral—says that women can't phone men? Poor Alex Bell must be rolling on this one.

The greatest compliment a man can receive is to have a woman call him on the phone. Just the fact that she cares enough about him to swallow that old-fashioned foolish pride and dial his number is heartwarming. I don't know of any man on earth who deep down doesn't appreciate a woman's call. And modern women call many men to socialize or as a part of their business duties every day. It's become as normal as breathing.

Let me add: HOWEVER! If the two of you are single and the other person already has a steady beau, to call them on a social basis would be intrusive and unwelcome (unless it's an emergency). Also, calling a married man at home is taboo (unless business or emergency related, or wife-approved.)

But other than these few common sense restraints, call men to your heart's content. We love it! And when you do call, don't complain or gripe about someone or something. A phone call from a lady should be sweet music to our ears.

Please don't call a man to check up on who he's going out with or where he went. He doesn't need Big Brother looking over his shoulder (or is it Big Sister?). And, if the guy is a baseball or football nut, don't call in the middle of the Super Bowl or the World Series games on television. Just a little consideration will go a long way and keep him on the phone a lot longer.

Okay! So you agree to call a man for the first time and you're nervous. What excuse should you use to call him, and what should you say to him? (Some of you liberated women who call men all the time might think this subject belongs to ancient history, but my mail indicates that it is a MAJOR problem still today, with widows in their 30's on up. So hang in there!)

As far as an excuse, you don't need an excuse. Just the fact that you want to talk to him is excuse enough. But if you are nervous and need some kind of excuse or "crutch," be creative! Ask him a question relating to his expertise in his business or profession. Ask him how to repair something in your home (you always have something that needs repair). You might even get him to volunteer to come over and handle the repair chore for you; if that happens, consider it an extra bonus. Once you get over the preliminaries, just carry on a simple conversation as you would at the office or if you were out to dinner with him.

Dear George:

"What is your opinion of a man who stands up a woman on a date? My girlfriends seem to have a problem with this."

A person who stands up another person on a date is about the lowest form of life on earth. These creeps are only concerned with themselves and don't have the slightest regard for the other person's time, dignity, or injured feelings. I've been stood up twice, so I know what a terrible feeling it is. It makes you feel hateful and revengeful. It's the pits.

There are only two valid excuses for a person to stand up another person on a date:

1. You are a victim of an auto accident or severe heart attack on the way to the date.
2. You are kidnapped by terrorists and whisked away to Lebanon.

Your girlfriends should spread around the names of the guys who stood them up, as a warning to other potential victims. It'll serve them right.

Dear George:

"I want to invite a man to dinner, but I don't know how to do it."

If it's dinner you are preparing in your home, that's easy. Just call him and tell him what you are planning to serve and that you'd like to share it with him. Any single man in his right mind won't need coaxing to accept this invitation. (However, if the dinner menu includes liver, Brussels sprouts, and tripe, get ready for a whopping rejection.) Be reasonably sure he likes the food you will be preparing. Or, better yet, ask what his favorites are and choose one to prepare for him. He'll arrive for dinner with a huge smile on his face. I know it. I have arrived smilingly dozens of times.

Now if a woman wants to invite a man to a *restaurant* for dinner, that's a horse of a different color. A good rule of thumb to follow is that the man should usually do the inviting for dinner in a restaurant. Chances are good that if he wants to dine with you, he'll let you know.

Again, there are exceptions to every rule. If both of you are already very good friends and, for example, it's his birthday or you want to celebrate some special event, then it's okay for the woman to invite the man. And remember! Nothing is more boring for a man (and for a woman, too) than to have dinner with someone you really don't care to spend that much time with, no matter who picks up the tab.

There are so many other happenings a woman can invite a man to besides dinner, events where both can feel comfortable, such as a walk in the park or on the beach, an artistic event or gallery showing, a condo cocktail party, and so on. There are dozens of these bona fide events to which a woman can easily invite a man where he won't feel like he is on the dole.

However, if a couple is in a one-on-one relationship, and they both have flipped over each other, then an occasional dinner on the lady is fine. But I still think it's best to find a good reason for it, such as the anniversary of their meeting or to celebrate a raise at work— something innocuous like that.

Remember! Our manhood is being challenged and assaulted at every turn nowadays. Don't let it happen at the dinner table too!

Dear George:

"I've been hoping for this dreamy guy to ask me out. Finally he called for a date, and I already had one for the same night. I told

him I'd take a rain check, but he never called back. Is it okay for me to call him?"

Let's face it. He probably feels rejected. Any kind of a "no" answer—even though it was legitimate—is a form of rejection. Some people can accept it better than others.

Many of us get rejected all day long in the business world. If we don't make the sale, it's a form of rejection. If our boss or our client or our customer doesn't like something we say or do, he or she lets us know about it right away—and it's another rejection. In a man's eyes, women are the last hope to save the day—after a day full of rejections. That's why it's so important that women avoid the "sound" of rejection when a man asks for a date.

And that trite old remark about the "rain check" doesn't help matters either. It's worn out.

I think it would have been much better to have said something like this: "I have a prior commitment that I can't get out of, but I'd much prefer to go out with you. Could you instead change the date to another night?" (Mention several alternative nights when you'll be free.)

First of all, this lets him know you really want to go out with him. And then immediately gives him a choice of two or three nights when you are free. That way, you will make him feel comfortable and wanted, not rejected. Chances are, he'll opt for one of your free nights right away, and you'll both be winners.

NEVER tell him that you can't see him because *you have another date with another man.* Make it sound serious—family or business—or you'll kill the whole deal. Here are some other excuses my research has turned up for not accepting a date that are guaranteed to turn most men off.

"I've got to wash my car." (Men think they are more important than your auto's cleanliness.)

"I've got to wash my hair." (Most men think you can get up a little earlier the following morning to wash it.)

"I've got to help my kids with their homework." (Until what hour? And why didn't you help them sooner, before it got to such a crisis stage?)

"I'm going out with my girlfriend." (To do what? Look for other men?)

"I'm too tired." (Would you say that if Leonardo DeCaprio called for a date?)

Ladies, be a little imaginative in the way you drop us poor guys, even if you have to tell a little white lie to spare our feelings. It's so important. After all, we're just a bunch of little boys trying to cope in a woman's world.

As for phoning the man in this letter, do it by all means. He showed he was interested in you. Now it's your turn to show you are interested in him.

Dear George:

"Why don't you tell your female readers not to wear a ring on their wedding finger if they want to attract single men. Several times I have bypassed some really nice-looking women because they looked like they had a wedding ring on, only to discover later—and too late—that they were single."

Agreed! Most single men—unless they don't mind looking down the barrel of a shotgun held by a jealous husband—will steer clear of married women and those who appear to be married. Some single women, such as waitresses and others who serve the general public, find it necessary to wear a phony wedding ring to discourage the would-be mashers. But there are plenty of other single gals who wear an ornamental ring on their wedding fingers that could easily be misconstrued as a wedding ring, or at least an engagement ring.

(Speaking for myself, whenever I have a date with a really "great" single gal who happens to wear a ring on her wedding finger, I never mention it to her. I figure that it keeps the competition from "hitting on her," and therefore, I know she'll be more readily available whenever I call. Sneaky, eh?)

Ladies! If you are in the market for a man, keep your wedding ring finger as bare as a hound's tooth. . . until Mr. Wonderful rings it for you.

Dear George:

"How long do you think is a reasonable time to be going with a man before marriage is considered? "

Why get married and spoil a good friendship?

Of course, there is no possible time frame for determining when marriage is right for you. However, your age plays an important part. If you are 16 years old, you've got all the time in the world. On the other hand, if you are 95, better get that ring in a hurry.

I think more important than how long it should take is how much you know about the other person. I know of so many second-, third-, and fourth-time newlyweds who discovered too late that they didn't know enough about their marriage partners—about his drinking problem, or her infidelity, or his temper, manners, habits, and so on.

The most important thing you can do is take the time to see your potential mate under all different types of situations BEFORE you tie the knot. Put away your rose-colored glasses and pay attention to him or her in everyday situations that you will encounter when married. It helps avoid not only the trauma of divorce, but also the double trauma of attorneys' fees. The old adage still holds true: Act in haste, repent at leisure.

I cover the importance of really KNOWING your date-or mate-throughout this book, so here are my first two examples of "dates from Hell." One woman was having dinner in a restaurant with her new found male "friend." She had to excuse herself to go to the restroom and when she returned he was *gone*! But the dinner tab was still there.

Another man informed his date that bed would follow dessert. This time *she* went to the restroom—and slipped out the side door and went home. Luckily, she had driven her own car—which is ALWAYS a good idea for a woman dining with a man she doesn't know very well.

As you progress through these pages, you'll see I have quite a potpourri of singles' incidents to report, and I interject them at random throughout every chapter. I do that on purpose to keep you alert and entertained . . . and maybe even to keep you *awake*.

I recently was noticing a group of married couples chatting at a long table in a lounge-women on one end and men on the other end-and it reminded me of a party I had previously attended. It was held in a gigantic home and as guests there were approximately 25 single people and about 20 married couples. The singles congregated in one end of the huge living room, and the marrieds split up on the other end—husbands in one "bunch" and wives in another "bunch."

The singles were all discussing their latest travel experiences, tennis, skiing and other interesting subjects that kept their conversations lively. Then it dawned on me: I wonder what the married couples are chatting about. So I sauntered over to "their" side of the room and stood with the men, listening to their conversations. Would you believe it? Their topic of conversation totally evolved around a new clothes dryer one of the men had purchased that day, and whether it was a two speed, four speed, etc., and the benefits of each. No wonder the wives set up their own conversation "bunch" because the guys were so boring. I quickly returned to the lively "singles" conversation.

The lesson here? If and when we get hitched again, let's keep it an exciting experience so the women will fight to join us and hear our interesting conversation . . . not just at a party, but also at home as well. It only takes a little effort.

Getting back to appropriate "singles" behavior: Here's a comment from one of my gorgeous readers how we men can improve. "Recently I met a man for coffee. His cell phone rang and he proceeded to talk with someone about his investments. I excused myself and went to the ladies room. When I returned he was still on the phone! (I should have walked out). Some days later I met another man for a drink. His cell phone rang and he chatted at some length with a relative. I consider his behavior rude and officious. Men: Turn off your cell phones unless it's a DIRE emergency."

It appears that this reader doesn't have much of a problem getting dates. It's too bad they're with inconsiderate guys.

But it's not just the men at fault. I can't count how many times I've been with women who interrupt our conversations to answer that damned cell phone. Usually, if their conversation isn't an emergency, and it lasts longer than 30 seconds, I'll simply ask the server for our check and I'm outta' there. Why waste time with inconsiderate people.

Continuing to look at *today's* singles, I thought it would be interesting to read what men and women look for in a date/mate. I conducted several of my many surveys among the many thousand readers of my newspaper columns and here's what the ladies look for, in order of importance. Attention Men: the following comes from many thousands of gorgeous single women and widows ages 30 and over. Pay attention! They all want, in order of importance:

1. Good sense of humor (this leads all my surveys)
2. Truthful and honest
3. Happy/fun loving
4. Caring/considerate
5. Financially secure
6. Intelligent
7. Positive attitude
8. Morals/spiritual
9. Emotionally secure
10. Fit/good shape
11. Affectionate
12. Healthy
13. Likes travel
14. Sincere

15. Easy going
16. Neat appearance
17. Open minded
18. Adventurous
19. Good dancer
20. Warm/Cuddly

Then I asked the ladies what type of man turns them off—one that they won't date. Here is a list of the top losers among men, in order of importance:

1. Alcoholic or can't hold his liquor
2. Man who smokes
3. Jealous/possessive
4. Couch potatoes
5. Wigs/ponytails/long hair
6. Stingy/cheapskate
7. Arrogant/bad manners

Since this is an equal opportunity book, here's what thousands of men look for in a date/mate in order of importance. The men also were age 30 and over.

1. Slim/trim/shapely/pretty/attractive
2. Good personality
3. Affectionate
4. Sense of humor
5. Fun loving
6. Honest/truthful
7. Conversationalist
8. Giving/caring
9. Intelligent
10. Employed/financially secure
11. Open minded

12. Romantic
13. Adventurous
14. Sincere
15. Good dancer

As I did with the women, I also asked single men and widowers what type of woman turns them off and they won't date. Here's their answers:

1. Women who smoke
2. Overweight
3. Users/takers
4. Gold diggers
5. Suspicious/untrusting
6. Game players
7. Unapproachable
8. Religious fanatics
9. Baggage (kids, pets, ex-husbands/boyfriends)

Now that we know what thousands of singles like—and don't like—let's keep this in our minds as we continue to examine today's "single scene."

I seem to have met or chatted on the phone with a surge of single gals—ages 45 and up, divorced and widowed—who REALIZE they must get out more and socialize more, but they don't do it because they don't have a convenient girlfriend to accompany them every time. They would rather die than go someplace by themselves where we single men might be.

Believe it or not, most of us considerate gentlemen understand and empathize with their feelings and we try to make your new experience as painless as possible. But we can't demonstrate our concern unless you gals SHOW UP!

Are you beginning to get the hint that the way to jump-start the rest of your life depends on YOU?

As I mentioned earlier, "singles" now outnumber "marrieds" for the first time in our history and 45% of the voters in national elections are "singles". Yet Republican or Democratic platforms have never even mentioned anything for and about "singles" or the inequity of the IRS tax code against "singles". But this is not a political book so let's get back to the FUN!

In the 30-35 age group, one-third of all men and one-fourth of all women are single because they CHOOSE to be single. They want to establish their careers, they want to see the world, they want to live a "wild and crazy" life before they do the domestic thing. These are possible reasons why people are marrying much later than just fifteen years ago. Then the average newlywed male was age 23 and the bride was 21. Now the new grooms are 27 and the brides are 25 on the average. More and more "singles" have other priorities before they say "I do". Many sociologists claim that these later-age "pairings" are caused by today's large divorce rate and singles don't want to make a marriage mistake!

Chapter Three

THE BIGGEST PROBLEM FACING TODAY'S WIDOWS!

I guess I should say *"problems"* because there are more than one. But don't forget: this is a *positive thinking* book and we look at problems as nothing more than *"opportunities in disguise."*

I think I can safely say that THE biggest problem for most new widows is their ATTITUDE! Adjusting back into single life can be a real problem for many people. And it continues to get worse every year for those who waste their early single years moping around or refusing to acknowledge they are now part of the "singles scene." Like it or not, folks, take it from a friend: you are *single!* Get into your new singles environment as soon as humanly possible. If you don't have someone to accompany you, then do it by yourself. Don't sit there in front of the boob tube and vegetate. That's wasting a good human being—YOU!

In the singles world, many of us tend to create our own problems because of our attitudes. I would say that the biggest contributor to a lot of widows' unhappiness is their *attitude.* Their attitude toward life, toward their fellow singles, toward society, toward women, toward men, toward just about everything they can criticize, condemn, and complain about. I've seen attractive women turn-off men in droves with their complaining or negative attitudes. And I have seen just as many men turn-off women with their defensive macho prancings, their attitudes of disgust toward women, their rudeness. . . their cheapness. What a waste!

First of all, it is vitally important to look at the positive side of life. If you look for what is *right* about things rather than what is *wrong* with them, I guarantee your single life will improve dramatically. This is the most important suggestion you'll get out of this book. If you have an attitude problem, change your attitude, and you'll change your life . . . for the better.

Other major problems facing widows/widowers is how to overcome loneliness, how and where to find a date-or reliable companionship, and how to get over the death of a spouse.

At this point, we're going to divide this chapter between males and females; and since it's the polite way to act, we'll let the ladies go first.

This Section For Widows Only!

O.K. ladies, let's get down to business. You already know that there is a shortage of men today. (It's not our fault). As women get older, this shortage can become alarming, with ratios of 2 to 5 women for every man. . . or more. Despite these odds, many of the newly single women I have talked with think they have to revert back to the days before they were married (no matter how long ago that might have been) to a time when they were popular with the boys or may have been the queen of the ball, with men fighting for their attention or affection. These women (my guess is 50 percent of newly single widows) seem to think that things will revert back to the way they were before their marriages. But what a shock they're in for! And the shock gets worse as the women age. (Remember, I said I'd be truthful!).

The newly single widow has usually put on a few years, and probably a few extra pounds and miscellaneous sags. She might even have a few youngsters at home. If you put them all together, they spell LESS DESIRABLE THAN BEFORE! Like everyone else, women change over the years, and if they are going to be well-adjusted widows, they must accept the fact that things have changed and *can never be the same as they were in the premarital days*. The average newly single widow may find very few GOOD single men fighting for her attention and affection. In fact, she may wind up fighting for THEIRS. (Wash my mouth out with soap!)

Every man is different, just as every woman is. Judge us as WE are.

Here's another problem many newly single women find hard to deal and cope with: women's liberation! With women's lib a permanent fixture on today's social scene, some of the customs, mores, and actions that were unthinkable a decade or two ago are considered normal behavior today—things like calling a man on the telephone, asking a man for a dance or a date, paying your own way (or even paying for his), driving yourself to a date, entering lounges alone, and going to singles parties and dances by yourself. I could go on and on, but you get the point. Women's liberation made it a different world out there, and you'd better accept the fact and learn to blend in.

The singles scene can be a very pleasant journey toward an interesting and rewarding period in your life, if you don't allow your "attitude" to erect a barricade.

An ancient Chinese philosopher once said, "Every great journey begins with the first step." For many women in today's single world that one step can be the most difficult action they can imagine. But once most of them take that step and see that everything is still all right with them, they quickly take their places in the singles world and eagerly anticipate each new day. I've seen it happen thousands of times. Try it! You'll like it!

Here are the results of a survey I ran in my newspaper column. It's how men think women can improve. (Don't fret ladies: I ran the same survey among women. . . coming up).

I got a whole bunch of suggestions from men ages 34 to 70, how women can improve. Here are the best of them. Remember, I just print them as I get them, so don't blow up. We all need improving. I include a few random comments to keep the criticism lively.

(From age 62 man) Stop playing those childish games. If your first impression is that you like us, then let us know it right away and we'll have a good time together for more dates. Later, if we turn out to be a dud, you can always turn us off then. But don't turn us off before we ever get a start.

(From age 60 man, married 3 times) Women should be honest, be complimentary and tell it the way it is. Keep it simple! (ED: but if she tells it the way it is, it may not be complimentary.)

(From age 34 man) Women need to be better "listeners."

(From age 66 man married twice) Tell women they can't get pregnant from kissing. Some women equate it with "going all the way." I think all single men should go on a strike for one year and not kiss any women. Then maybe they'll appreciate us and dump their old fashioned notions. (ED: Wow! I just print them as I get them! And you won't find me on the picket lines.)

(From 41 year old man) My father is 72 years old and just married a woman who struck up their original conversation. If she hadn't come over to him first (he's bashful), they would never have met and never have married. Tell women to approach more men that attract them rather than play hard to get.

(From a 61 year old man, married twice) If a woman would like to meet a certain man, she should make a move toward him. Rather than be aloof and have nothing happen, she should come over to him and start a conversation. (ED: as these two comments indicate, *MOST MEN* are too bashful or timid to approach a lady they haven't been introduced to. It's a real problem with lots of guys, and women need to come to our rescue.)

(From a 46 year old man, married once) Most women need training wheels. (?) When they become single again, they revert back to their teen years and think they need to start all over again with teenage thinking. They should mature and grow up.

(From a 44 year old man, married once) Why do women dress to attract us men, and then try to turn us off when we bite? They're a bunch of hypocrites if you ask me.

(From a 39 year old man) The telephone works both ways. Some ladies will never call a man for a lot of outdated reasons, then she'll call him on the carpet for not calling her. Women are plain unfair.

(From a 55 year old man) Women need to be more honest and down to earth. They all play stupid games and won't commit their feelings until you spend hundreds of dollars on them. Give me a straight-forward, honest woman and I'll marry her on the spot with no pre-nuptial agreement. (ED: But will she *want* to marry a grouch like you?)

(From a 53 year old man) Don't be so rude and inconsiderate. Women will interrupt men in the middle of a conversation to speak to someone else she hardly knows. They want to show they're in control. (ED: Even if the conversation is boring, it's still rude.)

(From a 51 year old, married once) Women should recognize that we're all equals and that they must EARN our respect, not think it's inborn in them.

(From 55 year old) Women should support their men more. They should realize it's a team effort. If she wants or expects more than he plans to give, she gives less and less. That's wrong. Proper balance is vital. That's the only way it works. (ED: What did he say?)

Another comprehensive survey I ran among men (and women later), gives an indication of what men prefer in the perfect woman. (Aren't they all perfect?)

A woman's looks (attractive, shapely, cute, etc.) was the number one requirement of men on a date, followed closely with the woman should be a *non-smoker*.

Next, he wants a woman with a *sense of humor*, and she must be *honest, intelligent* and *educated*. Then he also wants her to be *trim* and *physically fit*. She must have a *good personality,* be *fun/funny/ fun loving* and *active*. (So far it sounds like all gals fit the bill.)

Then his soul mate should like to *travel* (including day trips). She should be able to conduct an *intelligent conversation,* be *kind, financially secure,* have *poise* and be *sweet*.

The majority of side comments that were returned with this survey dealt with female GAME PLAYERS! So, naturally, I asked my female readers if they have ever "played games" with men. Here's what a few of the honest ones wrote (with my own thoughts at the ends). I can't determine if they are all "game playing" or if it's deceitfulness, coyness or dishonest. You ladies make the call:

"If he's interested in me, he should approach me. . . even though I'm totally interested in meeting him. But I can't show my interest!" (C'mon! This is the 21st century.)

"If I arrive on time for a date, I'll drive around the block several times so that I'm a little late. I don't want him to think I'm anxious to see him. . . even though I looked forward to this date for several days." (What a waste of gasoline.)

"I don't kiss on the first date . . . even though I'd love to jump his bones. I have to stretch these dates out to the max and make my moves when I determine I'm nearing the end of the gravy train." (At least she's honest about being dishonest.)

One "Lady" said that when she's on a date in a lounge, she'll purposely strike up a conversation with a strange man to show her date that he doesn't own her. She also thinks it makes her appear to be popular and desired by other men. (Most men I know would think she's "sick" and would avoid her like the plague.)

"I flirt with good looking men, and when they respond I ignore them." (Sort of like teasing a puppy dog.)

One man, a millionaire, said "you can tell if she's a game player if she's read the book 'How to Marry a Millionaire.'" (I claim the worst game players are those who pay attention to the rubbish in the book titled "The Rules," the game-players bible . . . the game of losers!)

"If a man won't give me at least 24 hours notice for a date, I will turn him down. Doesn't matter how busy he might be at work. I just want to embarrass or hurt the guy, or put him down for no other reason than he's a man." (Sick!)

Some men chimed-in with their opinions: "two women at a singles dance or party, totally engrossed in conversation with each other, oblivious to all the men around them" (Why don't they carry-on this vital conversation elsewhere, where there are fewer distractions? Why don't they pay attention to where they are? Lots of guys hit on this.)

"Women will dance with a stranger while on a date with me, because I don't do that particular dance." (Hope he steps on her white shoes.)

More than a dozen men decried women who will stand-up a man on a date. (Worst kind)

A big "no-no" among men is game playing women who respond to matchmaker ads or love connection newspaper ads with such evasive descriptions of themselves as "a gentlemen doesn't ask a lady her age" . . . "or her weight", or they state that they're "height and weight proportionate"...or "Reubenesque figure", all game playing subterfuges for something to hide. (Most men would rather go out with a totally honest responder, regardless of what it is she thinks she has to hide.)

Nearly all agreed that the worst game playing is pretend you don't want a date (when you really do.); Pretend you aren't interested in men (when you really are); Playing hard to get.

So ladies, I thank all of you for contributing so much to this book and admitting your game playing foibles to us poor, helpless men. My experience observing the singles scene for several decades is that GAME PLAYERS ALWAYS LOSE!

I'll close this segment with the way I opened this chapter, with a few examples of ATTITUDE problems that you might enjoy.

I ran numerous singles dances (the admission charge of $5.00 always went to a local charity) and I usually placed only 15 or 20 tables around the dance floor, even though I would get 500 to 1,000 singles at every dance. My plan was that if most people were FORCED to stand, they would mingle more—and that's what a singles event is all about. The bashful men, as long as they were forced to stand, might as well ask women to dance—and they did. Some of you might be thinking "what a meany this guy is," but it worked very well! At my dances and other singles events, many hundreds of singles met their future spouses, and many thousands met great dating partners. I forced them to! The proof is in the pudding, as they say.

But no matter how hard I worked, there were usually a handful of negative women who just HAD to complain. They wanted a table and chair in the far corners of the room where they could chit-chat with their girlfriends. HEY LADIES; you don't go to a singles party/dance to chit-chat with your girlfriends. You go to meet NEW friends. I usually refunded their admission price and they took the hint: complaining is a "no-no"!

Here's an example of an extreme negative attitude I encountered from an officious-looking woman. Every Christmas, I sponsored the largest singles Christmas party in my state—I did it for years and years and we raised thousands of dollars for charities, and the dance was always a huge success for all attending.

At one party, this woman asked me if she could tell me something. Naturally, I responded "of course you can!" And she said (quote) "This is the worst party I have ever been to" (unquote). I was naturally taken aback because she was there a half-hour before our scheduled starting time. The band was just setting up and the hors d'oeuvres were just starting to come in from the kitchen.

This is what I mean by "bad attitudes." Some are worse than others, but ANY negative attitude is BAD. Naturally, I escorted her to the door, refunded her admission charge, and wished her well.

Before we get to the next segment where we skewer the men, let's take a look at what men said their favorite sports, hobbies and interests were. This may give the ladies an idea of what faces them as they circulate among more men. In order of mentions, the men like:

1. Walking/Hiking
2. Movies
3. Travel
4. Golf
5. Cycling/Swimming
6. Fine Dining
7. Music
8. Arts/Theater
9. Tennis
10. Dancing
11. Reading
12. Football/Gym/Work out
13. Fishing
14. Gardening
15. Cooking
16. All Sports

I think we've covered just about the whole gamut of singles "opportunities" that await the gals. Now it's the men's turn in the barrel.

This Section For *MALE* "Singles" Only!

Before we tear into the men, let's pause for a minute with a few thoughts for widowers. The "single" male species appears to have more distinct differences than single females. These differences are especially noticeable when it comes to personality comparisons between men who are divorced and those who are widowers.

The widower who first ventures into the singles scene often becomes the hapless prey of aggressive women just waiting to spring the trap. I've seen many of these men blindly stumble into a relationship—and marriage—with someone they hardly knew. Just because they had been married practically all their adult lives, they felt uncomfortable without it.

It seems in too many cases, as soon as men become single, they become disgustingly CHEAP! I remember one widower who wrote to my column and said he was having trouble trying to meet his next "Ms. Wonderful" and could I help? He checked-out to be VERY wealthy, with no societal problems. So I arranged to fix him up with a very cute date in his town and he took her to dinner. The first thing he asked the waitress was if his 50 cent discount coupon from the newspaper was still good. Can you believe this? I can! Here he has a great date and the first impression he gives is that he's a total cheapskate. But that's not all.

As long as we are skewering men, how about this one? I sponsored over 1,400 singles parties of all kinds. In one town, I sponsored a weekly happy hour (live band, dancing, free LARGE hors d'oeuvres, 2 for 1 drinks)—admission two dollars for the American Cancer Society. Their chef approached me and asked why some men were coming in through the *back kitchen door*. (some women too!) He pointed out a few of these men and I asked why they came in through the kitchen and they said it was to avoid the $2.00 admission charge because they weren't sure it was really going to the Cancer Society.

What creeps these guys were! They were getting ten dollars or more worth of free stuff in exchange for a TINY charitable donation, but they just couldn't hide their cheapness. I've seen similar incidents dozens of times. Ladies! If you are dating a man with these cheapskate characteristics, be aware that he prefers "savings" over "smooching!" It's time to move on!

Here's another thing that bugs me about some widowers (and widows, too)—those usually over 50 years of age who get remarried. Many of them are so worried about whether or not the heirs in their own family are going to get *all* of *their* money that they treat their new marriage partners as a *drain on their heir's inheritance*. I have seen this in nearly half of every remarriage of widows and widowers. They are more interested in what they are going to leave their heirs than they are in having a wonderful second life with their new spouses.

And every one of these people explains it by saying that they think this way because their family is blood-related and the new spouse is an "accommodation" or a latecomer, or something else that makes the new spouse sound and feel like an interloper or, at best, a second-class citizen. I have even known some remarried people who pay their own lunch and dinner checks apart from their new spouse, even though they live and eat together every day. Can you believe it?

If you are in your later years and you are lucky enough to find someone to love you despite your infirmities or age or whatever, I think you should treat that person as you would like to be treated. And don't make them feel like they aren't appreciated or needed . . . because they are needed far more than a few bucks are.

And don't be afraid to leave your new spouse some big bucks if you depart this world first. After all, your spouse put up with your crankiness in your old age on a daily basis: Your kids didn't!

Now, on with my surveys. I asked my female readers ages 24 to 70 how men can improve. Naturally, I was flooded with suggestions, so I condensed the best of the most popular ones.

(From 47-year-old woman) Men have too much tunnel vision with their own careers and not a wide variety of interests; not enough balance in their lives. They should focus on being more interesting to talk to, and leave their jobs out of much of their conversation, and their former wives out of *all* of their conversation.

(From 42-year-old woman) Figure out what makes us tick. Don't think you know everything about us because you had a few failed dates. . . or a few failed marriages. We're all unique and special in our own way.

(From 37-year-old woman) Men should raise their moral values, be monogamous, honest and "old school." Take responsibility.

(From 28-year-old woman, never married) Don't lie! Be more self confident and less jealous. Be more caring and understanding of women. Also, don't cheat!

(From 50-year-old woman, married 3 times) Be more considerate, more romantic, more honest.

(From 70-year-old woman) Stop being grouchy and such cheapskates.

(From 61-year-old widow, after just breaking up with her five-year younger lover) Men should try telling the truth. Don't date two women at the same time. Don't be so critical of a woman's shape unless you're built like Arnold Schwarzeneger.

(From 63-year-old woman, married a bunch of times) Men who put women down to build their own egos should consider how they'd feel if she did this to them. Also, be more open and honest about their feelings and not just about "scoring," because being friends is more important in a lasting relationship than just "scoring."

(From 49-year-old woman) Be more sensitive! Be more grounded! Get off your ego train!

(From 42-year-old woman, married 15 years, divorced one year. Husband decided to date a 21-year-old instead.) Men should be more sensitive to a woman's needs. Be faithful and remember: you've also added a few more years and a few more pounds.

(From 34-year-old, never married) Men should learn to be forever romantic, treat us with manners, and still be independent enough to get their own beers.

(From 44-year-old, married once) Men should be more romantic, more old fashioned, respect our opinions, be a good listener. Physique doesn't do a thing for me.

(From 37-year-old, married twice) Don't be fakes. Don't mask your true personality until we find out too late that we're basically incompatible.

(From 28-year-old, never married) Be true to your word. If we make plans to do something, don't cancel out at the last minute. And if you say you're coming over at 6 p.m., don't show up at 8 p.m. Have more respect for us and our time schedule.

A big turn off with many, many women is the "macho" man. Here's the combined comments of thousands of women:

"He's totally in love with himself. He acts like he could care less for women (although in reality, he is constantly grandstanding before them). His attitude is that any woman he speaks to should appreciate the honor. He's pompous, arrogant and usually rude. He's "preened like a peacock," wearing all the mandatory jewelry. He's overly loud and boisterous, seemingly trying to be publicly obnoxious. A mustache is a requirement (though the gals quickly added that all men with mustaches aren't macho). If he ordered top shelf brands in the lounge, he seemed to want everyone else to hear it and appreciate his exquisite taste and great wealth."

"He'll loudly discuss how much he paid for his home, car, boat, etc. (whether true or fictional). He'll demean one or several women and discuss their faults openly for all to hear. He'll brag about the women he has bedded (although if the stories are true, they're all one night stands). He's an expert on everything. He's up on all the local gossip and wants to share it with the entire bar, whether or not anyone cares to hear it."

"On a few occasions where permitted he'll light up a cigar, unconcerned about the discomfort it is causing his neighbors. He'll bide his time until some nearby female gets herself so liquored-up that she can actually put up with him. He won't spend money on women, but if he does, he thinks he "owns" them. He'll try to impress people how much he can drink."

"He struts around like he has a corn cob stuck up his butt! (shame on you ladies!) He has a super ego and wants to be the center of attention. He is really a loser when it comes to love and relationships."

My researchers came up with this final advice for "macho" men (it should apply to all men); "do unto women as you would have them do unto you! . . . and then shut up!" (There go all my macho readers).

In another survey, I asked women the following two questions: "What do you look for in a man?" and "What type of man turns you off and you won't date?" I divided the ladies equally by ages: under 40, 40-60, and over 60. I had over 4,000 responses and the thing that surprised me was that the thirty year olds had the same values as the 60+ year olds. In fact, their answers are so similar that for the most part I can combine all the age groups. Whatever happened to the generation gap we used to hear about?

Of the personality characteristics most women look for in a man, guess which one was the most mentioned? Surprisingly, it was *"Sense of Humor."* That beat them all by a wide margin, all age groups. Secondly, women want men who are *"truthful/honest."* Next came *"steadily employed/financially secure."* Then in descending order, from all age groups, come *"happy/friendly,"* *"a gentleman,"* *"energetic,"* *"loyal/faithful,"* *"good dancer,"* *"commitment,"* *"caring,"* *"likes to travel,"* *"considerate,"* *"self confident,"* *"open minded,"* *"good listener,"* *"good in bed,"* *"good conversationalist,"* *"chemistry,"* *"treats her like a lady,"* *"good personality,"* *"mutual interests."*

As far as the PHYSICAL characteristics women want, the winner by a wide margin had to do with hygiene and appearance: they want their men to be *"neat/clean/neatly dressed."* Next they looked for a man's *"eyes"* and then he should be *"healthy!"* Surprisingly, no one mentioned that the man should be handsome or cute or good looking. When I asked them why they left this out, they all said that personality traits are far more important than looks! (So men! There's still hope for all of us!)

Now for the "turn-offs." These ladies showed no mercy, and that's good! They really let us have it! Again, all ages have basically the same answers.

The number one turn-off had to do with booze! A man who is an alcoholic, or gets belligerent, or can't handle his drinks is definitely the leader in male turn-offs. No question about it!

But following closely on its heels is a man who is *"jealous/possessive."* They really emphasized that this is a super large turn-off! Next came *"smokers"* and especially men who smoke cigars in public places (bars, restaurants.) They all consider it the height of inconsideration, so guys: light up that stogie on your front porch if you want to keep the women on your side. Next came the subject of *"hair."* Keep in mind, I didn't put any words in anyone's mouth and I didn't let anyone else influence them either. What you see is what I got!

The issue of hair got a little confusing. While they all were turned off by *wigs & toupees,* and all didn't like *pony tails* or *long hair,* when it came to facial hair, they were evenly divided: half liked beards and mustaches and half didn't. However, none liked men with a hairy back and they all hated guys with *nose/ear hairs.* It became a pretty hairy subject!

Another turn-off that really got the gals steamed was *"men who expect the gal to go to bed with them after the first date"* or expect it as payment for him buying dinner. Evidently, this sort of behavior is quite common, but won't be anymore after this survey!

These were all the most common turn-offs, pretty equally divided among women age 30-70.

Since we previously harpooned female game players, now it's

the male game players turn in the barrel. I asked the women about their experiences with male game players.

A lot of gals said the worst male game player is the man who pretends he really likes her but he really only wants to get her "in the sack" to add to his list of "conquests." It's devastating when she suddenly realizes this.

Another BIG problem is with men who say they are going to call her but never do. A few ladies said some men think they can mess around behind her back, but Heaven forbid if she does the same.

"He led me on with ideas of a great future together while he was out shopping for my replacement."

This one happens a lot: He takes her out on a date and then spends much of the evening schmoozing with other women, to show her how lucky she is to be out with such a popular guy.

One man gave a very classy lady a "commitment ring" (his words) which he reported to be a very valuable ring. When she learned it was a two-buck Zircon, she got rid of both fakes.

A lot of women commented on men who are super CHEAPSKATES! (I don't consider this as "game playing" since the game is usually over as soon as he reveals how cheap he really is. But since we're puncturing inflated male egos, here are a few of the many cheapskate tales I received.)

"He took me out for dinner and when the server brought the check, he surprised me by asking for separate checks."

"We met for a cup of coffee at a McDonalds and he expected me to pay for my own cup." (I'll enter him in the cheapskate's hall of fame.)

Two women said that when the server presented the bill, the men suddenly remembered they left their wallets home and depended on the women to pay for the dinners. They are both still waiting for their money back. Amazing!

A bunch of women complained about game-playing men who pretend to be filthy rich, but as the women sadly discovered too late they didn't have a pot to P—in nor a window to throw it out of. I even had one reverse of this. . . a wealthy man who pretended to be poor, drive a jalopy, gave an impression of near-poverty. The lady admitted that she was a gold digger and cursed her luck for giving-up on the guy and then finding out later that he was loaded.

So in the interest of improving male/female relationships, I did one of my usual "unusual" surveys, asking gals age 28 to 60 what "clues" or "body language" they give out that tell the man "he ain't it and he ain't gonna get it." Here's what I found out so far (with a few of my own embellishments.)

If she never touches your arm/leg/shoulder/knee, she may be purposely giving you the cold shoulder. (Take a cold shower instead).

If she watches a boring TV program while you're chatting with her, what bigger clue do you need. (You're even more boring!)

If she looks past you or over your shoulder at other men at the bar, don't leave her to go to the men's room. She may not be there when you return.

If she spends more time reading the menu than socializing with you, consider yourself her meal ticket.

If she sits with her arms firmly folded in front of her, this indicates she has set up a wall between the both of you.

If you detect a forced smile on her face when nothing is funny she's being forcibly polite.

If she always has a headache . . . well, we all know THAT one.

I hope this little survey will help all of us men learn about the feminine mystique. . .and when to walk out on the check (just kidding, ladies).

Chapter Four

HOW TO RELIEVE THE LONELY BACKLASH AFTER THE DEATH OF A SPOUSE.

One of the major problems in single life is that of loneliness. Here the media psychologists can describe how loneliness *acts on* your psyche, but they don't usually have *practical* answers about how to *eliminate* loneliness from your life. Widowed people don't need to be told how loneliness can affect them; they already know this better than anyone. What they need is to learn the best ways to *overcome* loneliness . . . and I hope that's where I can help. The loneliness problem can be solved with a little effort, as you'll see as you read on.

And even though I might sound jocular in many of my comments, you should know that I take very seriously that getting along in the single world as a new widowed person may very well be the most important thing you'll ever do for yourself.

The greatest joys I have ever experienced have come as a result of people who followed my recommendations and successfully got out of their ruts. Here is one example from one of my readers:

Dear George:

"I read your column all the time. I'm a widow and have been so lonely in my new city (I moved here 6 months ago), and I only had one friend. I finally took your advice and embarked on a 7-day Caribbean cruise for singles.

I met so many nice people from my area that I now have SIX good friends, and I'm not lonely anymore, I'm dancing, socializing, getting out, and enjoying myself as never before.

You are the cause of this, and I will thank you for the rest of my (happy) life."

When I received this letter, I framed it and hung it on the wall above my computer. It made everything that I have tried to do suddenly seem important and worthwhile. And that brings me back to my "impatience." I wish every widowed person would do as this reader did, and as quickly as possible, get out and socialize. Bury your preconceived Victorian notions. Take the bull by the horns and get off your duff. Get out into the world!

Loneliness is a huge problem . . . especially for widows . . . and more especially for senior widows. Many times I've talked to lonely women on the phone who were sobbing so uncontrollably that I could barely understand them. They seemed to hurt more than if they had a serious physical ailment.

Of course, adding to their loneliness problem is that the older they get, the fewer men there are in their age group to socialize with. By the time they reach their senior years, women outnumber men 2 to 1. It's a sad and serious problem.

When we look at the population figures, they explain the disparity. Men and women under 49 years of age are pretty much even. When they reach ages 50 to 64, the men drop off until there are about 90 men for every 100 women. Over age 65, we're down to about 65 men to every 100 women. Of course, these are national figures. In five states, men actually outnumber women. These are mostly in the sparsely populated "BIG SKY" western states and Alaska (125 men for 100 women), where nightlife consists of outracing the wildlife. As one lady put it: "the odds are good but the goods are odd."

But regardless of age and demographics, many women don't have the opportunity to meet single men because of the type of job they have, raising small children, and numerous other distractions. These contribute to the loneliness problem . . . as far as dating is concerned.

It seems that it would be easier to get over someone whom you divorced after a bad marriage than it would be to get over a spouse who died. But quite often that doesn't appear to be the case, especially for women—or especially for the thousands of divorced and widowed women I surveyed. Except for a handful of instances, newly divorced women seem to crawl into a shell of self-pity and isolate themselves from the rest of the singles world. They seem to reject single life as a disgusting distasteful way of life, even though they freely chose this path themselves. According to my survey, newly divorced men feel this to a lesser degree and are quicker to accept their fate than most women.

Widows and widowers, on the other hand, seem to more readily accept getting into the singles swing again. Certainly, they still mourn the loss of their loved ones, but once they face the awful reality that that person will never be around again, they accept the inevitable and socialize much more quickly and heartily. Maybe the reason for the differences between divorced and widowed people is that the divorcees, knowing that the "ex" is still around, may subconsciously hold out hope that they might rekindle the spark that got them together in the first place.

Dear George:

"How long should you wait after your husband's death to get out into the world again? My husband died 8 months ago (at age 49) after a lingering illness. Now I want to go to some singles functions, but my friends say it's too soon. They say I should wait a year out of respect for my husband. What do you say?"

I say tell your friends to mind their own business. I don't know who came up with that "one year" bit, but I've heard it many times before. It looks to me like it's more to impress the "living" than it is true respect for a departed loved one. How can you put a time frame on mourning?

I know many people who have mourned the death of a loved one for many years, and that's fine. But many others are ready to start their lives up again much before the year is up, and that's okay, too. In my opinion, it is up to YOU, not some friends who are only interested in appearances. If you're ready to resume living, then get going.

Remember in a previous chapter, I mentioned that the "single" ladies have to be CREATIVE if they are going to overcome the loneliness problem and meet new people? Here's an example of a truly creative widow who had a ball in her final years.

A trust officer of a bank told me about a widow who set up a variety of charitable trusts to be paid from her safety deposit box upon her death. She bequeathed half a million dollars to several charities, a quarter million to several others . . . really big time gifts. He was obligated by law to notify these charities of the largesse they could expect to receive. Naturally, all these charities invited this generous woman as their guest at various social functions and dances they sponsored as fund raisers, and she had a ball rubbing elbows with the rich and famous for several years. Upon her demise, the trust officer opened her safety deposit box to discover barely enough money to cover her funeral expenses.

St. Peter: watch out!

There are plenty of medical research projects that have shown the first year for widows is the hardest-physically and mentally. They seem to have more mental and physical problems than women who were still married and also women who had been widowed for longer than a year. But it seems they possess special "resilience" because after that first year, most of them bounced back and returned to normal. Also, these women who acquired many new friends lived the longest and happiest senior lives, and that's what this book is all about.

To try to get more widows into the social scene, I started *National Widows Week* the last week in June where I sponsored a number of free social hours and dances throughout the week. It worked quite well and it was exciting watching these lovely ladies, as young as age 38, get into the swing again. I loved it!

Many people say the best way to beat the loneliness problem is to get involved more in physical and social activities, such as dance classes, yoga classes, travel clubs, volunteering . . . there really are a lot of groups that will help overcome loneliness, but they don't know you're lonely unless you get out and avail yourself of their service.

I often hear from people who think of Christmas (and many other holidays and anniversaries) as a sad and gloomy time of the year. They spend their holidays longing for the days of yore, when they had their families around them. Now with family members gone, and no spouse, the loneliness becomes an extra heavy burden . . . especially during the Christmas season. But it doesn't have to be this way.

Many psychologists claim that the gloom around the holidays is a result of not longing for days of yore but of shorter days with less sunlight. Too much sun deprivation over a period of time affects our attitudes and can cause depression.

Every Christmas day when I'm alone, I like to dwell on the fun my grown children are having that day, in their homes, with their little ones. The fact that they are enjoying themselves brings me much joy. After all, I raised them to make the most of their lives, and now when they are doing just that, I can sit back and enjoy the fruits of my labors in raising them. Christmas and anniversaries are special times of happiness because I choose to look at them with a positive attitude.

I'm not going to tell you that I never look back a little longingly at those good old times, because I do. But I do it in APPRECIATION for the great times I was lucky enough to be part of, not in sadness that they're gone.

I think this kind of positive outlook is the only way to go. Some people are so negative and so down on everything, that they downright hate the approach of Christmas. And some take it to such an extent that they actually become sick (really) over the thought of the holiday season. In my opinion, these people are "sadness hypochondriacs," looking for a reason to be sad and gloomy. I've seen single people who previously had never felt any melancholy during the holidays suddenly dislike Christmas because their friends felt that way, sort of like the blind leading the blind. . . or the "sad" ruining the "happy." I think they need someone to step in and put a stop to it, rather than what I see so often where people seem to encourage this behavior.

I know of a group of elderly widows in the Midwest who get together every Christmas eve for a dinner party at one of their homes. They invite several married couples to join them, along with their children, to round out the generation spread. They enjoy their guests' companionship, of course. But more importantly, they relive Christmas through the eyes of the younger generation who are eagerly anticipating their Christmas bounty just ahead. As a result, these charming ladies thoroughly enjoy their Christmases.

Chapter Five

THE DIFFERENCES BETWEEN TODAY'S WIDOWS AND THOSE JUST TWO DECADES AGO

Women's attitudes have changed considerably—for the better—in the last 20 years to overcome loneliness. More and more women are realizing that THEY have to seek out the men, THEY have to be able to initiate the original conversation. It's a different "ball game" today.

Speaking of initiating a conversation, I was at a singles cocktail party in an upscale restaurant. I was just standing there minding my own business when a charming lady noticing I was holding a beer bottle, approached me and asked if I had ever tried beer from Croatia. What a great conversation starter! We had a delightful chat that included sights to see in Europe, famous beer spots in the world, etc. Remember when I wrote about being CREATIVE in an earlier chapter? This is a good example.

A lot of bashful women have written to me over the years about how to start a conversation with a stranger. One lady wrote me, "what can you say to a man you would like to get to know, as your opening line that has nothing to do with the weather?"

Good question! The first thing most women need is intestinal fortitude. Many are too shy or nervous or old fashioned at the thought of initiating a conversation with a strange man in the first place and will miss a lot of opportunities to meet her "Mr. Wonderful." If women knew how much we men respect and appreciate a woman who will initiate a conversation with us, they'd all do it. We don't consider you as being "hard up" or a "man hunter" or "brazen" or any of those ancient descriptions. We think you are a very special person who stands out in the crowd.

I checked with a few classy ladies what their best opening lines were to men they wanted to meet, and here are a few of them:

"I love your jacket (or shirt or tie). Did you get it here in town?"

"I couldn't help noticing your ring (or wristwatch). You don't see many like that, do you?"

"I like your moustache (or beard). Does it get warm in the summer?"

"You have such nice laugh lines (really wrinkles). Do you work outdoors?"

"You must be a reader of George's column. Have you read any of his books?"

"I read about a singles cruise to the Caribbean. Have you ever been on a singles cruise?"

"Didn't I meet you recently at another party? My name is _____. What's yours?"

"This is a nice party, don't you think?"

I'm sure you gals can come up with dozens of your own opening lines, but the main thing is they be a complimentary or positive statement, with a question at the end so that he is forced to answer, and he'll probably take it from there. Don't start off complaining about the weather or the traffic or some other gripe. I've had ladies say something like "boy, the traffic is sure miserable today!" or "the service is sure slow in this place" or "I've had it with all the rain we're having!" Thus, my first impression of these women is that they are chronic complainers and I don't want to pursue any further conversation with them. What a waste! If instead they had come on as pleasant, happy, positive people, we might have carried on an enjoyable conversation. The old saying "first impressions are lasting" is really true in these instances.

Even though the vast majority of letters I receive are from women inquiring about meeting men, men can still follow these same tips when trying to meet women. Give a sincere compliment followed by a question. But be sure the question isn't suggestive or doesn't make you look like you're coming on too strong, as it will probably turn her off. We men have to be much more guarded about what we say to a strange woman so that we don't scare her away.

On another occasion, a charming lady sent a drink over to my table. Naturally, I had to go over and thank her and chat with her, and it worked great! However, it's an expensive way to get a conversation started.

Here's another big change: women calling men on the telephone. I cover this elsewhere in this book, but here's a little thought I want to interject in this chapter: Ladies! Do you want to know what pleases a man more than just about anything? If a man takes you to dinner, or dancing, theater, boating, sends you flowers, or does something else nice for you (and you wish to see him again), it is vitally important that you telephone him or e-mail him the following day and thank him-again-for whatever it was he did. This not only keeps the lines of communication wide open, it also shows him that . . . 1) you are not just a user or a TAKER, 2) you don't play hard to get (which is for losers only), 3) you don't play games (which is for super losers, and 4) you appreciate his efforts to please you.

Ladies, if you'll follow this advice, I guarantee you will be a winner every time. And for those few of you remaining who will never call a man, remember Emily Post died a million years ago. Call the good guys PRONTO and you shall reap more than you sow.

Chapter Six

THE THREE BEST PLACES TO MEET OTHER SINGLES OR WIDOWS/WIDOWERS

Probably the most asked question among singles is where is the best place to meet other singles? Of the thousands of questions I have fielded throughout the years, this one accounts for about 90 percent of them.

The answer—a simple one—is, EVERYWHERE!

With the divorce rate and the death rate ending millions of marriages every year, it's almost as easy to meet singles as it is to meet marrieds; they're all over the place. But many singles have their heads buried in the sand and wouldn't recognize another single person if they jumped up and bit them (which, when you think of it, isn't such a bad idea. It's called a hickey).

Or we have those singles with tunnel vision, who *indirectly* pass up plenty of opportunities to meet other singles. What do I mean by meeting singles indirectly? Here's an example of what happened at one of my singles parties that may explain it. I've seen this same type of thing happen dozens of times.

A lady (I'll call her Sally) was hell-bent on finding a man at all costs. She was attractive enough, but too overly aggressive, and she had tunnel vision. To her, it was "find a man at all costs." At my party, she had been talking to another woman when she spotted two men chatting together. Ignoring (and maybe insulting) the woman she had been talking to, she made a beeline for the men and struck up a conversation with them, really trying to impress them. Overly so! As it turned out, neither man was impressed by Sally, and she was left more frantic and frustrated than before. What she didn't know was that the lady she had brushed off had an eligible male cousin and also had two good bachelors in her office, either one of whom she would have been happy to introduce to Sally. And if Sally had given the woman more time, she would have learned that she was planning a house party for single friends and would have been happy to invite Sally—but not after getting the brush off. Sally blew it with her tunnel vision.

THE BEST PLACE TO MEET SINGLES

Singles parties, events and dances are without a doubt the best places to meet your Mr. or Ms. Wonderful or just new single friends. Nearly everyone in attendance is there for one of two reasons: either to make new single acquaintances or to renew acquaintances with singles they already know. But the entire accent is on "meeting" and on "singles," so these types of events are your *best source* of making new friends. Now the only thing that's left is for some people to get up the *courage* to attend these parties, especially widows.

Dear George:

"When I read your last newspaper column in which you bawled out us singles for not supporting more singles activities, I felt you were talking to me. I'm 42 years old and widowed for 2 years. I just don't feel single.

"I did go to one singles happy hour at a prominent lounge, but I got so nervous by the time I got there that I couldn't open the door and instead turned around and went home.

"I can't find other widows who aren't afraid to go either. I feel like I'm stuck in limbo."

Going to singles parties and activities is like getting olives out of a bottle. The first one is the hardest of all, and the rest come easier. If it'll help, belt down a double scotch first. Believe it or not, this fear is experienced by probably 90% of newly widowed women.

Here's how to overcome this "first time fear." Get two or three women or men to accompany you the first time. They can be your relatives or neighbors or fellow workers, and they don't even have to be single. You can go with a married couple as support; the main thing is to go with someone you know whom you can lean on. After you've been at the party for a while and begin to feel at ease, move around on your own and notice what's going on and watch or listen to what the other guests are doing or saying. Chances are, depending on the type of party, everyone else is either dancing or conversing, or both. You've still got your friends to return to as your "crutch" in case you have an anxiety attack, so move around the party on your own and become relaxed.

Sometimes I get the feeling that people (especially women) think singles parties and activities are nothing more than wanton sex orgies where women are devastated by leering, lecherous men as soon as they enter. Maybe there are those types of parties; if so, I wouldn't blame anyone for avoiding them. But in all the thousands of singles parties that I have either run or attended, I can honestly say that I wouldn't hesitate to bring my mother to any of them (except for the fact that she's married and my dad would give me hell).

Dear George:

"I have been single since my husband died 2 years ago, and I am shy about getting around men because I was married when I was 18. We were married for over 45 years, and I'm so lonely. I would go to some singles parties, but I don't want to appear to be man hunting. I am only seeking companionship.

"I will try to find courage to go to a singles event. I don't dance but am willing to learn. Should I take some dancing lessons? Please advise."

You can have just as nice a time at a singles party by meeting other single women with whom you can share hobbies and interests . . . and companionship. And no one in his or her right mind at a singles party would look at you as being a man hunter,

as you call it. This is the 21st century . . . not the Victorian era.

As far as dancing, it would be a good idea to learn some of the basic steps . . . but here again, a lady friend can teach you these in a few minutes. However, if you do decide to take dancing lessons at a professional studio, beware of the dance instructor "charming" you into buying more lessons than Madonna ever had. Only spend what you can reasonably afford.

Not to get off the subject of singles parties, but this letter reminds me of another letter I received from a woman who took dancing lessons from a real "sharpie." I cover this more thoroughly in the chapter on "dancing", but let's look at her letter now.

Dear George:

"I thought you'd be interested in an experience I had taking dancing lessons. I went to (bleep) dance studio, and my instructor was very charming. He sure did talk me into buying $3,000 worth of dance lessons. He said that he was going to make a beautiful dancer out of me and that we were going to be a dancing couple. Have your readers beware of dancing schools. I have quit the school. And I'm not a beautiful dancer."

I heard from another woman who got "romanced" into buying over $10,000 worth of dancing lessons. Wow! That's $5,000 a foot. Before signing up for lessons, it's best to check references from previous students and the Better Business Bureau. It's much better to be a poor dancer than to be poor. But back to the singles parties.

Dear George:

"I recently moved back into town, and I'm determined not to fall into the doldrums trap of boring routines this year. I'm at loose ends as to what to do with my time and life. If you think singles get-togethers would welcome a vibrant 55 year-young widow with wide business, social, cultural, and political interests, I might like to try them."

It has been my philosophy that everyone who attends a singles party or event should attend with the idea of what they can contribute to the party rather than what they can take from the party. In this way, we all become "givers," and everyone wins. You sound like you could contribute a lot, and I'm sure you would be most welcome from the first minute.

But a word of caution: At your first party, be observant and keep a lot of your experiences—and your opinions—to yourself. Don't start off as a person who knows it all and wants everyone to know it. You'll get plenty of time to discuss your wide range of interests at other parties . . . like maybe the third or fourth one.

Dear George:

"How can we be sure that the men we meet at singles parties are respectable and trustworthy?"

You can't, not until you get to know the people in attendance over a period of time. But that's the same with married parties, too, isn't it? Maybe even more so.

We all know that one or two "weirdos" will always manage to slip into just about any party ever given, whether singles or marrieds parties. I personally know of some very restricted church singles parties, very sedate and very solemn, that were attended by the worst "creeps" in town. And the same thing with private parties in homes, private clubs, art galleries, and so on. In other words, weirdos are here to stay; there is no way to completely eliminate them from attending any parties they want to attend because no one instantly recognizes them as being "strange" until it's too late.

I suggest you follow these simple rules when meeting a man for the first time, whether in church, a lounge, a private home, or anywhere:

> Don't give out your last name to a stranger unless you know it's all right. (This prevents him from looking up your phone number and address in the

city directory or the internet and bothering you on the phone, or stopping by your home when you least expect him.) And, of course, it naturally follows: Don't give out your address or phone number unless you get to know him **very well**.

Don't let a new male acquaintance walk you to your car alone.

If a new male acquaintance asks you for a date and you want to date him, tell him you'll have to confirm it with him later, after you check your calendar, and ask him for HIS phone number and address. If he doesn't have a telephone or his local address is a nearby motel, MOVE ON!

On your first date, meet him in a public place and drive your own car or take a taxi. This way, if things don't work out, you always have transportation home.

Don't be snowed because he's a good dancer. Pay attention to everything else about him. Some of the biggest con artists are the best dancers. Conversely, some of the nicest guys are the lousiest dancers (for example, former President George H. W. Bush). Contrary to popular feminine opinion, *dancing isn't everything.*

I know of a widow who made arrangements to meet a man for a first date in a public restaurant; she drove her own car. As it turned out, after one drink he became totally obnoxious and started to make passes at her. He let her know in no uncertain terms that bed would follow dessert. She excused herself between the salad and the main course to go to the ladies room. Instead, she made a beeline for her car, and drove home. She wouldn't have been able to escape as easily if she had depended on her new date for transportation.

It's smart to plan ahead.

Many churches and temples have singles groups and I think these events can be great places to meet like-minded singles. But you should check them out with an open mind.

Dear George:

"You always talk about meeting singles, but what's wrong with meeting them at church activities? I think it's a better atmosphere."

I agree it's a better atmosphere. But you can't cuddle up with atmosphere on a cold winter night, because that's about all you'll find at most of the church functions I've attended . . . and I've been to a bunch!

It seems many church groups don't attract the exciting, modern-day male or female because the church parties are usually so monastic, so puritanical—yes, even boring. They appear more as proselytizing endeavors than "parties." Singles go to a party for a *vacation*, not a *vocation*.

And, usually, church group singles events seem to border on immaturity. Some events include games that we played in grammar school, ice cream socials, box lunches (where the women end up sharing their lunches with each other because not enough men are attracted to the idea), hayrides with no hay, and religious skits. I could go on and on. One church event I attended featured "group" projects in which people were divided into separate groups to solve a Bible riddle or some similar "problem." I guess the idea was to get to know the opposite-sexes in a small group a little better. But what happens if you have your eye on the gorgeous brunette in another group? You're stuck the whole evening in the group you got assigned to. By the time the evening is over, the brunette has lined up a date with someone in her group and leaves with him. It happens.

When a church group has a breakfast or dinner function, everyone enters and takes his or her seat at a table set for about fifty. So you only get to meet the people on either side of you—and maybe across the table. Church groups for the most part don't plan their events to appeal to your average single persons or their needs.

But don't criticize without offering a solution. Following are some suggestions for how I think church-sponsored singles parties should be planned.

If it's going to be a sit-down meal, have it start out in a "cocktail party" type of atmosphere in which everyone mingles—on their feet—for about 45 minutes before they take their seats for the meal. Guests can walk around with a cup of coffee or soda pop while they mingle with the other guests in attendance.

Fill out a name tag for everyone as they enter. And put their business occupations under their names. It's a great conversation starter.

The next thing these church party organizers have to decide is whether the party is going to be a prayer meeting or an honest to goodness singles party. If the object is to attract people to these parties and get them to come back and bring friends and grow larger, then they've got to go the singles party route. I have seen many, many singles turned off when they found that the singles party was more of a ruse to get these people into the sponsor's church and attend a church service. If I want to go to a prayer meeting or a church service, I've got plenty of churches around the corner I can attend much more conveniently. When I go to a singles party, I want it to be a "party." Besides, I think a church can accomplish more with a lot of "short blasts" of religion done discretely and spread over many parties, rather than one big effort at one time, never to see the guests again.

Dancing is also important if you are going to get the guests back on a regular basis. I know of one church group that didn't allow dancing because they said it was immoral. So instead the singles got together for what they called a "bundling" party, where the couples wrapped themselves together in a blanket out on a moonlit lawn.

Now that's my idea of a great singles party! You avoid all the miscellaneous buildup and head straight for the sack.

To heck with dancing. From now on it's bundling for me. I wish I could remember what denomination that was.

Dear George:

"As a professional organist, I have played for many weddings. I always ask the bridal couple how they met. Many of them met in church-sponsored activities, at friends' homes, in college, at political meetings, at sports activities, even on blind dates. Frankly, I'd rather my daughters were introduced through mutual friends than by a bartender. Wake up Girls! There is a world outside the dark bar scene."

Whoa! Hold it! I never said women SHOULD go to bars to meet more men. I only said they're a good PLACE to meet men. It would be nice if we all could meet our mates at the events you suggest, but let's be pragmatic. If we all waited to be invited to one of the functions you suggest, we'd never leave home; there just aren't enough of them geared to singles mingling.

Many church-sponsored singles parties I've attended have 50 women and 10 men in attendance, and they all seem to congregate in "hives." It's usually a very cold atmosphere, as though the sponsors didn't think we were even worth the bother to hang a piece of colored crepe paper to let us know this is a special party event.

And someone always manages to introduce the 70-year-old men to the 30-year-old women, and vice versa. You get the feeling that you must be the most hard-up person in the world just for attending.

And how many cups of fruit punch or tea can one consume and still keep smiling? No one running these church parties seems to care or bother to take us singles seriously.

I've tried the Sunday morning coffee-after-church get-togethers, but they are basically for married couples. I feel like a hypocrite if I try to use these types of church socials for my own private life enhancement.

This letter writer wrote, "Wake up girls! There is a world outside the dark bar scene." I wish instead she had written, "Wake up *guys*, and support and attend all the quality singles activities that are sponsored not only by churches but also by other groups for the benefit of all of us singles." That's the biggest problem: Men don't attend these activities because no one makes a concentrated effort to attract them. And if the men don't attend, the women won't either . . . and the entire effort is doomed.

One last thing: You can't have the age disparities at these church functions like the ones I've seen so many times. You can't mix two or three generations and expect anything to happen. Music preferences are different. Tastes are different. Conversational subjects are different. If you organize church singles parties by age groups, you'll get lots more attention and interest.

We all need GOOD church-sponsored singles activities. I'll be the first one to shout it from the rooftops (or should I say from the "steeple" tops). But the organizers have ro realize that not everyone in attendance has aspirations of becoming a monk or a minister. Of the hundreds of church parties I have attended, it would appear that Reverend Moon and his followers have more fun at their functions than we do at the average church-sponsored singles function.

So until someone decides to run church activities more effectively and pay attention to the special needs of single people, the principal places to meet your Mr. or Mrs. Wonderful can be found on all these pages.

Here's another letter I received from a lovely lady named Toni describing her efforts to get local churches to host single activities . . . more specifically singles breakfasts on Saturday mornings. She says she's a born again Christian and doesn't do the dance/alcohol/tobacco scene. She proposed to a number of churches that they sponsor singles breakfasts and they never even bothered to respond to her. She even complained to Billy Graham and Pat Robertson and they ignored her also. She says that they all sponsor programs for unwed mothers, baseball teams, summer camps, etc., but won't even answer her when she discusses "singles" and their need to socialize.

So I got an idea! Cut out this page and next Sunday take it with you to church. When they pass the collection plate, give them this instead of your money. If they get enough "pages" and a little less money, maybe they'll get the message!

Before I leave the subject of church/temple sponsored singles parties, let me interject this thought: My biggest complaint is that there are over 200,000 churches and temples in the U.S. and only about 5% sponsor anything for singles. All the rest of the church buildings sit idle for most of the week when they could be used for worthwhile singles activities . . . what a waste.

———————— · ————————

Here's a 21st century innovation that is taking the "singles scene" by storm. *Speed Dating!* It's a great way for busy singles to meet lots of singles in a short period of time. I think it can be really great . . . as long as the sponsors maintain adequate controls.

If you have never participated in a speed dating encounter, I recommend it. A few places charge an exorbitant entry fee and that can turn-off a lot of potential "good" participants. Every single person isn't so hard-up that they'll pay any price to meet another "single", so the high-priced events turn me off cold. But if you have to pay an admission of $10.00 to $25.00 for a *very well* organized event, it could be the best bucks you'll spend. Especially if they draw equal numbers of both sexes.

I have participated in a number of speed dating parties and I have always met women who have become great friends. (And so did the women since I became a great friend of theirs). Here's how the average "speed dating" works: Single men and women are assigned a number. Then the women sit at tables and the men join them for a 5 to 7 minute introductory chat. At the end of that time period, the organizer rings a bell (or blows a whistle) and the men move to the next table and to the next single woman. Meanwhile, if the previous woman would like to meet him again, she enters his assigned number on a form. And, if he wants to meet her again, he enters her assigned number on his form. This goes on from table to table until everyone has had a chance to meet and chat with everyone else. At that time, the party organizer collects the male and female forms that had been filled in by the participants. Any numbers that match (where the male and female participants *both* indicated that they would like to meet each other again), the women are given the men's private telephone number for her to follow-up on. (If you read this far in this book, you *know* it's O.K. for women to call men. It's not even a big deal anymore.)

However, if you both don't signify that you want to get together at another time, then nothing further happens and full names or telephone numbers are not disclosed. A sociable person can usually end up with five or six people who agree they should spend more time with each other, which is why speed dating is so successful.

I once planned to organize the world's largest speed-dating contest where everyone would chip-in five dollars to a charity to participate. I was going to limit the encounters to only two minutes since I knew I'd have thousands of participants. But I couldn't find a convention center or arena large enough to accommodate us, at a low rental cost that wouldn't deplete our charity's income. Alas, I had to abandon the idea . . . for now!

———————— · ————————

Other great singles meeting places are at singles "clubs". I'm not referring to the social singles clubs that try to rip-off lonely singles with large initiation fees and large monthly dues. Those are more money-makers for the organizers than they are good places to meet singles. I'm talking about the "themed" clubs such as bicycle clubs, travel clubs, sports clubs, ski clubs, hiking clubs, diving clubs, even bridge clubs. Usually all the members have some sport or hobby in common, and they usually can effect substantial savings when they participate in the event they concentrate upon. Sports clubs and other "themed" clubs can be great, if they are well organized by caring sponsors.

I'll close this segment with another letter from one of my female readers.

Dear George:

"I have been reading your articles for over a year now and finally decided to take you up on your offer. I always look forward to your article. I have often imagined joining singles gatherings but would always find an excuse to keep me from going. The truth is I am chicken. Finally, three weeks ago, I got up my nerve and went to a Wednesday night Holiday Inn party. First I circled the parking lot, then parked my car and proceeded to the door. Just as I was approaching the door, I turned back. That's when I said O.K. girl, get a grip. As I was ready to get back into my car, I saw a lady pull up and park. I waited and as she approached I asked her if she was going to the singles night. She said yes. Boy, was I happy. I then asked if I might walk in with her as I have never been to a bar alone. She was amused by it all and said of course, they are all a bunch of nice people and I will introduce you. We walked in and she introduced me to a few people at the bar and I sat down, started conversing with the neighboring crowd and before I knew it, there were five men around talking to me. Suffice it to say that I had a lovely evening. I saw someone I had met before and a very nice gentleman asked me to dance. We danced very well together, I might add. Everyone there was very friendly and courteous.

"You were right! All you need is to bring a smile and be sociable, and the rest sort of takes care of itself. My advice to the single ladies

who are as frightened as I was is: **Nothing Ventured, Nothing Gained.**"

But we're getting ahead of ourselves with this "bar scene" bit. But at least you are seeing that the number one best place to meet singles is at SINGLES EVENTS!!

THE SECOND BEST PLACE TO MEET "SINGLES"

Hold your hand over the rest of this page and see if you can guess where the second best singles meeting place is.

Are you thinking MODERN? NEW AGE? Isn't it *obvious*?

O.K. You've made your guess, now lift your hand and see how you scored.

If you guessed "internet dating", then you win a merit badge (or something like that) because by far, the second best place to meet (or at least chat with) singles are all the internet dating/meeting sites . . . and there are millions of these sites.

In the good old days—not too long ago—we could join "Love@ aol.com" and other websites at no charge, and e-mail our choice of potential mates and swap messages also at no charge. It appears those days are gone forever. Now the average matchmaking website costs $24.95 **a month** to be able to contact the persons of your choice. It's a half-billion-dollar a year business. Sure, many offer a *free look* at anyone and everyone on their sites, but if you want to *contact* these people, you must first sign on the dotted line. So when they advertise FREE sign-up or FREE access to thousands of dates, that's all you get is the sign-up and access to *look at* their photo and bio. Communicating is not free! The way they advertise it seems to me like a cyber rip-off. If you go to all the trouble to sign-up, they figure you're not going to waste that effort . . . and you're going to join their site.

At last count approximately 40 million people use these matchmaking websites *daily* and the number of match-making websites is tremendous. I went to Google and under "Matchmaking" they have 16,000,000 listings. So, it's easier to enter "matchmaking sites"; they have only 4,400,000 choices. It would take the rest of my life to scroll through this number. And, it's the same with Yahoo! Under "online dating" they offer 113,000,000 choices, and under "matchmaking sites", they only have a paltry 3,500,000 listings, at the time I checked this chapter out.

They can introduce you to a wide range of people or to a very targeted market of potential dates such as Doctors, Lawyers, Ivy League grads, Jewish, Catholics, Muslims, tall, short, millionaires... just about every variety you can imagine. The more picky you are about whom you want to e-mail, the higher the monthly subscription cost.

But beware of a few cyber pitfalls: fully one-third of everyone using these matchmaking websites is MARRIED. They're shopping around for a little action on the side, and if you don't want to be that ACTION, be wary. Also, be aware that many of the participants post a photograph taken umpteen years ago. Nearly everyone lies about his or her age. That's no big deal, as long as they chop off only a couple of years.

And nearly everyone lies about his or her weight. Men can easily lop off 30 pounds at the touch of a keyboard. No shame! No guilt! It's the weight they hope to reach if they ever start that diet they've been planning for years. But women are more elusive. If they're concerned about a weight problem, they sidestep it and won't state their weight. In this regard, they are more honest than men. Instead, they'll use terms like *"weight and height proportionate," "weigh a few extra pounds," "slightly overweight," "full figured," "Reubenesque,"* or *"it's not what's outside that counts but what's inside."*

All this translated means that she's heavy set. Many don't bother to list their weights at all. The question of weight is the most sensitive, but we must remember that some people prefer a mate to be hefty, just as others want him or her to be slim. Honesty is the best policy; sooner or later you're going to have to face the music, and it can be embarrassing to be caught in a lie.

In doing my research for this chapter, I ran several different personal ads on different websites. One of them requested, among other things responses from petite, slim ladies. The first e-mail I received was from a woman on the East coast who was five feet three inches tall and, in her words, "height and weight proportionate." It took me several e-mails to pry out of her that she weighed 163 pounds. Some people might say that's not height and weight proportionate!

I also wanted to test whether there is any danger in being entirely trusting with my respondents, so to four of them, sight unseen, I gave my home telephone number. Two called me back, but I guess the others thought it so strange that I'd do this that they never called me. Incidentally, one who called me lived a hundred miles away, and we made arrangements to meet halfway for a delightful lunch. She was cute and bubbly and a perfect date. But the fact that she or I would have to drive a hundred miles every time we wanted to get together with our busy schedules, made further dating futile. This is why I consider computer matching better for persons living in large towns or metropolitan areas with lots of potential *local* e-mail dates.

The other respondent who telephoned me in answer to my "slim" personal ad described herself as being "curvy" and said she looks like actress Mary Tyler Moore (who is very slim and trim). She pushed very hard for us to meet for a few drinks. Her photo on the internet looked young and pleasant and "slim," so we set up a meeting place. What a surprise I got! She weighed over 300 pounds. She explained that she was about to go on a diet and she was a lifetime Weight Watchers member. You just can't trust all the photos displayed on the internet, male or female.

Now let's look at some of the results my research subjects experienced on the internet. One man placed a short ad on a cyber bulletin board looking for a travel companion. A woman who lived a thousand miles away responded to his ad, and they chatted for a while. After determining that they both seemed compatible, he flew her to his home in Orlando, Florida. Unfortunately, she brought along her 10-year-old son, who was a total terror. The young son caused immediate difficulties and disruptions that the man admitted he couldn't put up with. So the lady responded, "That's okay! We'll visit Disney World," which she and her son did. The trip wasn't wasted for them, but it sure was a waste of time and money for the hapless man. Think of how much he could have saved if he had responded to only LOCAL women.

One lady (who only appreciates men with rock-hard butts) asked men for their photos standing up. No one complied. (Several men asked women for their photos standing up and got the same results).

Another lady responded to a gentleman's personal ad and sent him three pages of e-mail. He was looking for the silent type and he figured she must talk a lot. Nothing came of that one.

One man I talked to who preferred petite women thought it was ungentlemanly to ask a woman her weight and height, but he was exasperated at all the women who beat around the weight bush. So now he requests "dress size" and feels he's being a little more polite. And it sort of catches some of the women off guard; a few of them perhaps think he wants to buy them a garment of some kind, and they readily divulge it. He only continued e-mailing those with small-size dresses.

One lady with her young son moved to the United States from Latvia and couldn't speak English. But she quickly learned the value of the internet and ran a personal ad on AOL. A gentleman responded, and they eventually made arrangements to meet each other in person. At the meeting, she brought along her young son to interpret for her. End of romance!

I heard a few men claim that some of the women answer their e-mails with a lot of griping and complaining about their past experiences, or past husbands, or anything else they can find to be negative about. Naturally, that is the last these women hear from the men. After all, NO ONE wants to get involved with a chronic complainer—male or female! What a waste of good e-mail!

One man, after exchanging a number of e-mail messages with a woman, finally felt guilty and confessed that he was an incurable alcoholic and a woman beater, and she shouldn't have anything more to do with him. She didn't.

A man in his 70's ran a billboard ad looking for a lady to travel with him in his $200,000 RV. As you might expect, all of his 70-year-old respondents inquired whether his motor home had two separate bedrooms (with locks on the doors).

One lady who met with several of her e-mail friends reported that the photos they sent to her were at least 10 years old. A few men had the same comment.

Many people, even after a long e-mail relationship, won't disclose their home address. Most just give a post office box, and a few give an office address. This is a good idea: you never really know who is at the other end of your computer. Caution is ALWAYS the best policy. And if they are convicted felons, child molesters or other creeps, you would never know it by the glowing accounts they give of themselves. A word to the wise is sufficient, as the saying goes.

Now. . . A word of caution! Relying on the internet for dates can cause you to become a "Professional Dater"!

I describe a professional dater as one who continuously e-mails potential dates on the matchmaking websites. They endlessly sit in front of their computer screens e-mailing the heck out of the ads they have pulled up, or answering replies to the ads they themselves have placed on the same website.

A person who runs an attractive ad with an attractive photograph can expect anywhere from one to five new responses PER DAY. These responses can be from all over the country but will usually be local people. Now here's my gripe about this whole computer matchmaking business: after exchanging e-mails for a period of time (often as long as one month), they may agree to meet each other in person at some public place, and rather than *working hard* at making that first date blossom into a better relationship, they seem to treat the date rather lethargically and matter-of-factly, knowing that no matter what happens, when they return home from this date they'll probably have half-a-dozen new date offers awaiting them in their e-mails boxes. And many of these professional daters have been doing this for *as long as five years*!

Having this backlog of potential dates causes lazy, jaded daters who lack the incentive to expend the extra effort needed to make their present date work. Believe it or not, when I suggested to some people that they are becoming professional daters, most admitted their guilt but they were hooked like an addict and didn't know how to-or want to-get out of it. (Maybe we need to set up a D.A.—daters anonymous). Many admitted they just go through the motions of dating, all the while anticipating their return home to the comfort of their computers. Or they nit-pick the heck out of their date because he/she is not 100% perfect. They become introverted, socially lacking . . . even boring.

I e-mailed a number of professional daters and I also met and talked with other male and female professional daters (though none described themselves that way). Besides their take-it-or-leave-it attitudes, the alarming trend I noticed is that in 99% of the ads they ran on the internet matchmaking sites, and in their replies to me, they only discussed WHAT THEY WANT! Very, very few offered any idea of WHAT THEY CAN GIVE to a relationship. That's sad! It appears that the internet is cultivating a generation of TAKERS rather than GIVERS. Read the ads and you'll see what I mean.

It seems to me some of these "professional daters" can become unsociable and introverted. A political scientist at a prestigious University seems to agree. After researching the potentially negative effects of the internet, he wrote: "When you spend your time on the internet, you don't hear a human voice and you never get a hug." Amen!

I responded to a number of matchmaking ads that have been on the internet for more than TWO YEARS! Some up to FIVE YEARS. WOW! The fact that they haven't found a proper match among the hundreds of e-mail responses they have received during this time seems to support my claim that they have become professional daters and probably don't expend the effort needed to build a relationship! They could be trapped in the euphoria of anticipating the continuing number of prospective dates awaiting them when they get home from the date they're on.

Whenever I suggest that we meet face to face right away, I discovered that the unwritten law of internet matchmaking requires that you exchange up to half a dozen e-mails before the lady would even consider a meeting. "Hey! We're not getting any younger! Why the delay?"

But they all insisted on delaying a face to face meeting, even though I answered all their dozens of questions the way they wanted. Some even ran out of new questions to ask me . . . but still the delay. They probably were working several dozen guys at the same time and couldn't squeeze me in.

Some women ran two or three different ads with different e-mail addresses. The more fishing lines in the pond, the more fish you are going to catch.

Most of those who bragged about their great sense of humor seemed by and large grouchy, mistrusting and humorless. A few were simply searching for new recruits to their churches, a blatant proselytizing effort.

One man was really ticked-off at the whole idea of internet dating. He called these professional daters, "professional wanna-prove-I-can-get-a-date-but-don't-really-want-it" women. Obviously he must have had some really bad problems with e-mail dating. He even went so far as to castigate these women for playing mind games with this comment: "What is the purpose except to feed her ego?" Wow! Strong words. But an indication of strong frustrations possibly caused by some person's lack of "tact." When communicating with others on the internet, since there is no verbal communicating, your choice of wording is critical.

The professional daters I have met, instead of getting out of their homes and working at getting a date, take the easy—and lazy—route and sit at home e-mailing scores of potential dates, 99.99% of which will never work out. That time might have been better spent meeting someone face to face at a singles party or activity locally.

But, back to success stories:

A petite 54-year-old listed (with photo) on at least a dozen websites when lots of them were free. She let me read and count some of the hundreds of e-mails she has received. I gave up at number 91. She's had more than 2 dozen marriage proposals, more than 50 men traveled to her city to date her. She's had countless original poems dedicated to her from suitors living in nearly every state, plus England. The men were as young as 30 years of age, too! She swears by this computer matchmaking! (But why hasn't she settled on ONE man? Maybe she's developed a habit of "looking" and can't break it!)

One lady who had a very fuzzy photo in her profile, cut 20 years off her age and evidently thought she had to dress the part of a 50-year-old woman. Have you ever had a gray-haired 70-year-old great-grandmother show up for dinner in short shorts and a bare midriff blouse? It was startling! But at least I didn't have the horrible luck one man did. He said his computer love match turned out to be a transvestite. Ouch!

Seniors and baby boomers are increasingly depending on the internet for companionship. Some estimates quote figures as high as 30% of all personal ads are placed by singles over 55 years of age . . . some of them widows who have figured out how to operate the computer which their deceased spouse usually controlled.

Here's a hint for these seniors: when you are posting a photograph, use one that looks happy, pleasant and smiling. I have seen so many scowling, angry, grouchy-looking photos of seniors that it's a real turn-off. Take a new picture . . . and look happy!

Many of these matchmaking internet sites are becoming so popular that they now *require you* to pass a PERSONALITY test or face rejection. Some require a college degree, some require you to be recommended by another member of their site, some will simply screen your responses to the numerous questions they pose, and reject you for unspecified personality reasons. (Isn't it terrible to be rejected before you ever got the chance to ask someone for a date?) Oh well! It happens a lot. One website rejected over 80,000 applicants.

Many websites will check out everything about you . . . except your marital status. Some even advertise on prime-time network television. It's becoming so lucrative they can afford these exorbitant advertising costs.

If you like to live dangerously, there are a few matchmaking websites where you can correspond with prisoners incarcerated in penal institutions. There even is a site to match you up with male convicted killers on death row. It must be for those women who don't want a long term relationship . . . I guess.

If all my ramblings in this section have convinced you to try the internet-or upgrade your present profile-go for it. But don't forget! It's still only the SECOND best place to meet other singles.

THE THIRD BEST PLACE TO MEET "SINGLES"

This is where I get most of my criticism, mostly from unknowledgeable persons with closed minds, who depend on outmoded stereotypes to lead their single lives. But I have broad shoulders so I can handle the heat. The third best place to meet other singles is in UPSCALE lounges (bars).

Dear George:

"Where is a good place to meet nice men? I've heard that the bar scene is not where it's at. Where can a woman go?"

If you want to meet men, you've got to go where they are! Oftentimes, that happens to be in a lounge. You've got to play by their rules if you are seriously searching for Mr. Wonderful. And women going into a lounge is not such a big deal anymore (except in women's own minds).

With women's liberation here to stay, it is very common to see today's modern woman stop for a relaxing drink after a hard day's work . . . and why shouldn't she? Men do! Aren't women entitled to partake of the same pleasures and pastimes? I personally know hundreds of nice, respectable, proper women who often stop at a lounge for a brief respite, any one of whom I would be proud to bring home to mother.

And I also know hundreds of good looking respectable, reputable businessmen who regularly frequent lounges, many who go there for one main reason: It's the only place they know of to look for their Ms. Wonderful. When you stop and think about it, there probably is no better place, on a day-to-day basis, to meet a lot of new single acquaintances than a quality lounge. These new acquaintances can usually lead to invitations to house parties, sports outings, and other good things. But the original meeting in many cases takes place in a nice, quality lounge.

Now, I'm not trying to make alcoholics out of the singles world, because you can drink fruit juices, soda pop, and plenty of other drinks that are non-alcoholic. Fifty percent of bar sales today are non-alcoholic. Today's smart lounges know how to increase their revenues without increasing their alcoholic drink sales: They serve "mocktails"! These are colorful non-alcoholic drinks that look exotic, have a variety of tastes, and one can feel at ease and enjoy sipping a mocktail while socializing with others. In addition, many of the old standards—mai tais, margaritas, pina coladas, vodka tonics, etc.—can be prepared alcohol-free and they still taste the same. If you haven't visited today's upscale lounges lately, you're in for a pleasant surprise.

And I'm not talking about the bars that have the wet T-shirt contests or the free ladies night promotions. These places seem to draw the leering goons who think that every woman who walks in the door is fair prey. I'm talking about upscale lounges populated by upscale people. And to be an upscale person doesn't mean that you are filthy rich. It means that you are well mannered, couth, considerate of others' feelings, sociable, and friendly. If you fit this description, you'll feel comfortable in any upscale lounge.

When you try out a nice lounge, don't expect to hit pay dirt on the first visit. Don't be in a big rush to meet ANY man. You've gone this long; a little longer isn't going to hurt. It takes time and patience. Don't get discouraged if the first man you meet doesn't turn out to be Mr. Right. Keep trying. As the old saying goes, "You've got to kiss a lot of frogs before you find your Prince Charming." At least you're in the right hunting grounds.

Pick out what appears to be a pleasant "business person's" type of lounge. That means one near large downtown office buildings, or one near a suburban office complex, or one on a busy street normally traveled by working people on their way home from the office. Just put your own common sense to work, and you'll find a place that you will like, as well as one that an upscale person with similar tastes to yours would like. And, of course, I'm talking about visiting the lounge during the *evening* happy hour or late evening . . . not the morning or afternoon hours. Otherwise your Mr. Wonderful might turn out to be Mr. Lush.

Dear George:

"I still can't get up enough nerve to go to a singles party or happy hour in a bar or lounge. Isn't there some other place for us shy ladies to gather?"

How about a convent? I get your same comments all the time, and I still say that the first time you attend is the most difficult. Once you see that everyone else is the same as you are—all in the same boat—you'll quickly become at ease, and the rest of the visits you make will be duck soup. I've seen it proven over and over.

I've also heard a number of women (and some men) say, "I don't do the bar scene," or "I'd never want to meet a man (or woman) in a bar." I say BUNK! Granted, the so-called "singles bars" were pretty hokey, but they're out of style, and I say good riddance to them. But there are tens of thousands of neighborhood lounges, business persons' lounges, and other quality-type lounges that are excellent places to frequent . . . especially during happy hour.

If the lounge serves hors d'oeuvres, so much the better. Bachelors who are tired of restaurant food and don't like to cook (and the silent majority of us bachelors don't like to cook our own meals) will often get much of their sustenance and variety at the hors d'oeuvres table. I call it a "bachelor buffet." It's the sociable way to get some food into us without the boring, long drawn-out routine in a restaurant (where, by the way, we already eat five or six hundred breakfasts and lunches every year). It's a pleasant change from the humdrum of eating alone.

Happy hour usually runs from 5:00 p.m. to 7:00 p.m., Monday through Friday. I personally have met more than a hundred women at these bachelor buffets, and I know of many women who have met just about as many men.

People who regularly stop at a particular lounge on their way home from work soon became a "familiar face" in the establishment and will find themselves striking up conversations with other "familiar faces." And that's the thing that good relationship-starts are made of.

A word of advice for the women reading this: Be calm! I've seen many women sheepishly enter a lounge, nervously scan the crowd for 2 seconds, and then hightail it out of there like a scared rabbit. I guess they are really just plain frightened and that's too bad. Come in ladies and join the party. But don't creep in. Enter as the welcome guest that you really are.

I recall once being in a lounge after work during a Friday happy hour. I was sitting at a table with several locally prominent businessmen when a woman—about 35 years old—poked her head in the door nervously, scanned the lounge for no more than 3 seconds, and then hurriedly departed. It just so happened that this lounge was owned by a good friend of mine, and I didn't want to see him lose any business, so I chased after the woman and asked her why she had left so quickly. She answered that she was totally nervous about going into the lounge in the first place and, since she didn't see anyone she knew, she was going home. I told her that with the small amount of time she spent peering in the doorway, her whole family could have been sitting there and she wouldn't have spotted them. I introduced myself and insisted that she join me and my friends for a beverage. I suggested that it would calm her down and make her feel more at ease. I practically had to drag her inside, but she finally agreed.

I introduced her to my table guests and ordered her a beverage. As it turned out, she had had some business dealings with one of the guests at my table, and they both had a number of mutual friends. She soon became relaxed as they chatted merrily along.

I next introduced her to the owner of the lounge, the cocktail waitress. . . and just about everyone I could think of. I made her feel at home as best I could. From that day on, she felt completely at ease and returned nearly every Friday after work (and maybe other times). She frequented the place for over a year and became acquainted with lots of people; in other words, she became a familiar face.

Nearly a year and a half after I dragged her into this lounge, she married a man she had met there. As far as I know, she's still happily married to this day, and that's been more than 15 years now.

Many women have told me they don't like the shady characters they meet in bars. My advice here is to *change bars*. And as I stated before, you can meet shady characters at just about any singles (or marrieds) function you attend. So, don't be misled or drop your guard just because of the party location. The SMART shady characters know they will take on an air of respectability when they attend church-sponsored events or other so-called "private" singles gatherings, masking their true character. And women at these types of events tend to let their guard down, and when they do...zingo! The shady guy moves in, and Lord knows what can happen. I recommend that women be just as skeptical at church and private functions as they are in lounges—because lounges don't have a monopoly on "jerks."

Get to know the lounge owner, the bartenders, and the waitresses. Many times they can steer you away from the "creeps" and introduce you to the good guys.

On your first trip to a lounge, go with another woman—single or married doesn't matter—she's only there for moral support. There's strength in numbers. But remember: A man will be much more hesitant about striking up a conversation with two women than he will with one. After you get to know and be known in the lounge that you have targeted, go alone and give the new "familiar faces" a chance to chat with you one-on-one. Also, go easy on the alcohol. It blurs your judgment. And if you are driving, go especially easy or you may end up looking for Mr. Wonderful in the slammer. Also, remember, half the drinks sold are non-alcoholic. Where else can you get a choice of pineapple, cranberry and other juices?

Dear George:

"I agree with you that one of the best places to meet men nowadays is in a lounge. But where do we go? How do we go about it? How do we meet men? What do we say?"

As far as how women do it or what they say to someone in a lounge depends, of course, on what type of woman they are— whether they're the outgoing type or the shy, quiet type. But the first and most important thing for women to know is that they should sit or stand—*at or near the bar*. If they hide themselves at a table in the far corner of the room, they're dead! Preferably, they should look for an empty seat at the bar, near someone of the opposite sex and in their approximate age group. And if there is only one seat next to him, ask him if the seat is taken. He'll probably respond that the seat is not taken, and this usually breaks the ice. He'll probably carry the conversation from there.

Here's a true scene I recently observed in a neighborhood lounge in a large city. I was sitting at this fairly deserted bar, when a lovely lady entered and sat about six stools away from me. Soon after, a man came in and sat around the bend in the bar, about two or three seats from her. After a few minutes had elapsed, the lady commented to him about the "handsome smile lines" he had in his face and asked him if he worked outdoors all his life? He told her what he did for a living and they started talking. By the time I left, a half-hour later, they had become comfortable friends and had even made a date to go fishing together. I'm ashamed to say that I eavesdropped on their conversation. But I did so because she was so smooth at instantly winning a new friend. In fact, the man actually had a load of wrinkles on his face, but she turned them into "handsome smile lines." She said something positive and pleasant, and the conversation was off and running.

Some of you women are thinking, "Well, that's okay for the younger generation, who find it easier to talk to strangers. But how about those of us who are 30, 40, 50?" Well, the lady I referred to in this story was 73 years young, and the man with the smiles lines was 67. Surprised? Don't be! It happens all the time. If you want to strike up a conversation, do the following:

> Don't start off by complaining about the weather, or the traffic, or things like that. He might have endured complaining clients all day long and doesn't need to listen to another complainer. . .especially during his free time.
>
> Don't clunk down a huge saddlebag of a purse on the bar, taking up all the room. It makes it look like you are planning to camp out at the bar for the weekend. And don't put your purse on the empty seat next to you. It will defeat the possibility of a potential new acquaintance sitting next to you. If you don't have a small purse, then lock the "saddlebag" in the trunk of your car.

Don't let a stranger buy you a drink unless you REALLY want to spend more time chatting with him. If you accept his drink, chances are he's going to zero in on you and get his five bucks worth of conversation. And if he's a crashing bore, your stuck . . . at least for as long as the drink holds out.

Don't be pushy. If a man doesn't appear to be interested in talking with you, then leave him alone. There'll be other days and other guys.

Speaking of "pushy," here's a story that happened to me. One day as I was driving down the street, I suddenly got a number of brainstorms that I just HAD to get down on paper before I forgot them. A nearby lounge was the only place where I could write, so I went into the bar with my pad and pencil and began writing notes furiously, before I forgot all these wonderful ideas I had. I was obviously totally engrossed in what I was doing, when an obnoxious female came in and sat next to me. She unloaded her saddlebag all over the bar and demanded a drink from the bartender. Then (even though she noticed that I was writing like mad) she started to strike up a conversation with me. I tried to be polite and would nod or give her a quick comment to the string of complaints she was heaping on me about the weather, the traffic, and everything else under the sun, and then I'd return to my writing. Finally, she got the hint that I was busy and had to finish what I was doing. So she complained to the bartender that "some people don't have manners enough to talk with a lady," obviously referring to me.

I guarantee that this woman will NEVER meet a wonderful man who will become attracted to her, because she doesn't know how to be wonderful herself. She only cares about what she wants, to the exclusion of others.

I have heard hundreds (maybe thousands) of women say they would never want to date a man they met in a bar. I have dozens of case histories to refute this thinking, but how about this one for openers.

I organized a weekly singles happy hour in a medium size city, and I listed it in my newspaper column. A charming lady decided to take me up on my challenge to go visit it alone. That same day, a well educated widower decided he would give the "bar scene" a try, at my urgings. Guess what happened? They both met each other for the first time and decided to go someplace else for dinner. That was just the beginning. Approximately 4 months later, they both invited me to their engagement party aboard the 52 foot yacht he bought her for an engagement gift. I went! I was there! If they both hadn't kept an open mind, they'd still be alone. After they married, a short time later, they spent a 6 month honeymoon cruising the Bahama Islands on her new yacht.

And for those who think only uneducated losers do the bar scene, this man was a graduate of England's Sandhurst Academy (their version of West Point) and was a fabulously successful businessman.

Some upscale PEOPLE don't always go to *upscale* bars: Some visit working men's bars, and it's no big deal. (I don't want this to sound like I spend my whole life in bars, but I do a lot of research there if that's the topic I'm writing about.) Anyhow, I was in this working-man's bar discussing business with the owner when I noticed an elderly lady sitting *alone* at the *bar.* She was dressed impeccably, her hair coiffed stylishly and she wore just the proper jewelry. She was dressed as she would to attend a tea at Buckingham Palace, but she was in this lowly bar. So, naturally, my interest was piqued! I asked the waitress about her and here's the scoop: She was an 88 year old widow and made up her mind that she wasn't going to waste her life alone. She took a taxi to the bar. And either her 65 year old son would pick her up after work (after she'd had one or two beverages) or she would take a taxi home. Her reasoning was that since she had all these expensive frocks hanging in her closet, why not wear them instead of just leaving them in her will. So she did.

Also, I noticed many patrons would come in and give her a hug or a kiss on the cheek and inquire about her day . . . just "pleasantries" because she had now become a "familiar face" in the bar. In fact, when the patrons sat near her, they all seemed to adopt new manners and decorum while in the presence of this elegant lady.

You readers know me by now. I couldn't sit still. So after observing her for a while, I went over and did my little "interview" job. She said that she felt a little nervous the first time she entered the bar (it was not her type of UPSCALE lounge). But, everyone proved so friendly that she got over her fears and visited the bar two or three times a week to say hello to her many new friends. When I asked her why she did this, her answer was so prolific I had to write it on a napkin so I wouldn't miss a word: "I have a lot of life to live, why not live it!"

Whenever I would visit the bar after that date if she spotted me she would come over and touch my arm and remind me of our original conversation. A real classy lady who shared her "elegance" with average people. I mention her on all the talk shows that I am on as a tribute to her memory because she never made it to her 90th birthday. I want her elegance and unselfishness to endure in these pages for many, many years.

Dear George:

"I'm a "young senior (in the 50's-60's bracket)." I don't do the bar scene. Everywhere I go, I lower the average age by a decade. Every club and church supper group is packed with people in their 70's and 80's. Where do people my age congregate? The bar scene is frequented by alcoholics and heavy drinkers and is not a good meeting place in my opinion. I'd like to see you address this dilemma in your column. Sincerely, Anonymous"

First of all, if she doesn't do "the bar scene," how can she know they are frequented by alcoholics and heavy drinkers. A totally self-destructive, negative attitude. I personally know thousands of men and women who have attended my "bar scene" parties and who sip a beer, a wine or a soda all night long. Not exactly heavy drinkers! (And that's one problem: they usually are such *light* drinkers or teetotalers that the bar doesn't make enough to cover the band costs and I have trouble getting bars to sponsor singles nights with dance music.)

At my recent party "bar scene," there were over 500 singles in attendance. I didn't see one person who acted out of place. All were perfect ladies and gentlemen.

And I hate to tell this lady how many times I've seen the "neighborhood alcoholics and lechers" looking so holy in church Sunday morning. They're bound to show up ANYWHERE, so don't condemn the bar scene. Maybe the time has come for all of us to discontinue stereotyping people and places just because it gives us a sense of righteousness. Let's instead accept everyone of whatever age for whom THEY are, and if they turn out to be losers (it happens), simply move on. It's not a big deal if we don't make it one. (This is beginning to look like a "sermon". If I were writing this sitting astride a horse, you could call it my "sermon on the mount.")

I don't mind that she didn't sign her name, but the fact that she doesn't give her age and instead says she's in the "50's-60's bracket" gives me the idea that she might have something to hide or maybe is a little less than honest. . . with herself!

On behalf of all the single men who will stop in an upscale lounge after work to avoid the rush hour, or to delay going home to a lonely, empty house, and instead hope for some social interaction... (wow! What a long sentence). . . I invite all you upscale women to try it a few times. You can enjoy a non-alcoholic fruit juice if you prefer. If, after only four visits, you haven't met a super guy or felt like it's your private place to relax, then I will personally invite you for a beverage (on me) so we can figure out what the problem is.

Chapter Seven

OTHER GOOD PLACES TO MEET SINGLES

Even though I state that these are the "other good" places to meet singles, don't be misled. For some singles, these "others" may be the numero uno best places to meet, but I usually follow the average success stories and go by the number. Here are the next three best places in my research.

Lonely Hearts Ads In Magazines

"Lonely hearts" personal *newspaper* ads are a dying breed. But these same "lonely hearts" personal ads placed in targeted magazines can become a bonanza of great singles mingling and meeting. A female reader of my column wrote me about her experience placing a "Personals" ad in a national yachting magazine. She and her late husband had enjoyed their boat and she missed the nautical life and comradery. She received 17 letters form her ad, all from single men who owned various size yachts. She called half of them, met a few of them, and spent six months on the high seas with the best one of them. She swears by these "targeted" personals ads in magazines.

When I mentioned her story in my newspaper column, I received a flood of similar success stories. Men and women who placed "personals" ads in other magazines directed to their favorite pastime such as flying, scuba diving, water skiing, bicycling, etc. reported great results as well. All the respondents were interested in the same sport or pastime as the person who placed the ad, so good compatibility was quickly established. All the feedback I received from my readers was definitely POSITIVE. (I like that!).

Cruises

Dear George:

"Are ocean cruises a good place to meet women? I've heard pro and con."

It's very easy to meet women on a cruise ship on the high seas, mainly because they don't have anywhere else to go once the ship leaves port. The one drawback is that when the cruise is over, the woman returns to her hometown, which is usually located in another state, so you don't accomplish much in the long run.

However, in spite of this, I thoroughly recommend singles cruises in general, since there are usually plenty of single people aboard ship. Read on.

If it's your first cruise and you're not accustomed to attending singles parties or dances, I'd suggest you get your feet wet by attending some sort of singles get-together before you go. It will help you feel more comfortable on the cruise, since you'll better know how to act or react, and you'll get off to a good start, without wasting valuable time.

I have organized 28 singles ocean cruises, and my favorites are the gigantic luxury liner cruises to the Bahamas, Mexico, Bermuda, Hawaii, Caribbean, and so on. They have plenty of dancing, sunbathing and activities. And every cruise ship has a singles party the first evening out of port so that all singles aboard can meet each other (or at least look over each other). It gets the cruise off on the right foot.

The main reason I prefer very large cruise ships over the smaller vessels is that they are more stable in the water and don't rock and sway as much. It's not worth being on a cruise if all the single women are laid up in their staterooms seasick and all the single men are barfing over the rail.

The minimum cruise time should be 4 days. Any cruise less than that doesn't give you enough time to survey the situation and set your sights on some lovely young thing (or handsome hunk, for you gals).

And don't forget! Single women on a cruise are just as interested in meeting men as we men are in meeting them. So there is less pretense. Let's face it. No single person takes a cruise just to stare at the ocean.

I've seen a number of great relationships—even marriages—result from singles cruises. And those who didn't end up in a serious relationship nevertheless had a great time during the cruises. I recommend cruises for singles of all ages.

Let me mention one type of cruise that is becoming very popular lately. I'll call it the "happy widow" cruise. These cruises recruit widows and other single women as passengers and guarantee them a certain number of dances each evening with a number of different male partners in their age range. Naturally, the women pay a premium price for this "dance/dating" service and, judging from the number of women who take these cruises, they don't seem to mind it.

The men who are recruited to be their dancing partners get to go on the cruises gratis, and, in addition, are given from $25 to $100 a day for pocket money. The men's only obligation is to dance with a certain number of women each evening, usually 6 to 10 women. Then, when the men have fulfilled their obligation, they can spend the rest of the night (in addition to the days) mingling with the rest of the passengers on board. A few cruise lines require these escorts to accompany the ladies in the daytime as well, or even to show them the sights on shore at various ports.

The cruise directors and travel agents who put these cruises together usually screen the men quite thoroughly to be sure they know how to dance, know their manners, and don't mind dancing with all types and sizes of women—at least once.

This might seem like it's a good deal for the men. But after hearing tales about some of the verbal abuse that is heaped on them by some of these "happy" widows, they are forced to dance with,

I don't think I'd like the job, at least not until they also screen the "happy" widows.

On one of the singles cruises I organized (all were 8 day cruises), a woman in her 40's met a man in his 50's. They agreed to get together after the cruise had ended and within 6 months were married. They seemed like two teen-aged lovebirds as they made plans to go on another cruise as husband and wife, only this time it was a 105 day cruise around the world.

I met them after they returned and both enjoyed it so much they're planning another cruise. Wow! If you can *happily* live with your spouse in the cramped cabin of a cruise ship for 105 days—and want to do more—you are REALLY COMPATIBLE! See? Success stories are all over the place! Get out and create your own success story.

Singles Clubs

In every city, town, and hamlet there probably exists a so-called "singles club," where supposedly lonely singles can gather and socialize with other singles with the same tastes and of the same age group for a nominal annual dues. Do they succeed? Read on, McDuff!

Dear George:

"I'm tired of the bar scene. My church doesn't have a singles group, and I can't afford dating services. I have heard about singles clubs. What do you think of them?"

I don't think much of many singles clubs. I have found that in a lot of them they are run by domineering people with strong maternal instincts who like to boss their flocks around and take charge of other people's lives. Their demeanor usually chases away the *good* males and females, and often all that are left are those who can't make it anywhere else.

Quite often the club members act as if they are privileged people who are superior to "nonclub" people. A lot of them drive me nuts. However, as with everything else, I have to qualify my remarks. If the singles club is formed for a good reason or provides an extra service that the members couldn't get otherwise, then I think they're great. As I mentioned, ski clubs, bicycle clubs, scuba diving clubs, travel clubs, and other *specialized* clubs afford the members special activities or group discounts that make membership a good deal. Plus, the members get to meet and associate with other people of similar interests. I agree with and wholeheartedly endorse membership in these types of singles clubs. In fact, I love 'em!

Clubs that benefit charities and worthy causes are also good; they form a pool of volunteers who are ready and willing to help out in various fund-raising endeavors. I also heartily endorse these kind of clubs. If there is one in your town, join it!

It's the *social* singles clubs that leave me cold. Although I do know of several of them around the country that are well organized and run with the members' best interests at heart, the vast majority of those I've heard of or have attended have actually been *detrimental* to the members' well-being. I realize the importance most women place in dancing—men too—and a lot of these social clubs provide this outlet for their members. That's okay, too, if it stops there. But I've seen many instances in which even these club dances and "socials" become so inbred after awhile that all the members know in advance who to expect to be in attendance at each affair, and they tend to shun any newcomers of their own sex, for fear of competition.

In this regard, belonging to the singles club becomes stifling and actually *inhibits* the members' chances of getting out and meeting new people. The singles club member becomes a prisoner of his/her own club.

Dear George:

"As a woman, all the singles club parties I've been to have about 10 women to every man. Are there singles MEN'S clubs around that I don't know about? Where do all the men go?"

They obviously don't go where you go. And if there's a singles club for men, I don't care to know about it.

It's an age-old problem that just keeps getting worse . . . the lop-sided ratio of single women to single men in the world. This problem carries over to the vast majority of singles clubs; there are far too many women enrolled and far too few men. It sometimes can be embarrassing, especially for men in senior citizen clubs, where they are swamped with women the moment they enter the party, each woman looking for a dance partner. As I said before, "social" singles clubs leave a lot to be desired, for both sexes.

Dear George:

"I'm happily married, but I read your column always with pleasure. I wish I had the kind of help you give way back in 1980 when I was trying any way possible to meet new friends. My suggestion for people wanting to meet new people is to join an organization and become a volunteer in places where they will meet all kinds of new people. I used to go to the park and donate my time working (mostly with men). You can also meet some nice people giving your time to the Red Cross, Salvation Army, etc."

Good idea. It's like having your own private singles club that only YOU know about.

I know of many good social singles clubs around the country, but I also know of many that are mainly designed to rip-off the lonely single person. Before joining a club, check out their officers thoroughly and be sure the dues you pay are easily affordable.

I stated earlier that we all must be POSITIVE thinkers, but I did have to point out a few negatives to help you avoid certain pitfalls. So, to close this segment, I'll state POSITIVELY that most sports, travel, business, charitable, etc. singles clubs are GREAT! Check them out. And most Church social singles clubs are GREAT, too. Now at least you know what to expect—and look for.

* * *

Now to divert our attention for a minute: A long time ago, I received a short poem from one of my readers that I'll share with you.

> "With care they tottered down the aisle,
> and then their vows were said.
> These two who waited for the day,
> they could afford to wed."

So I had to try my own hand at this poem stuff:

> "But those who rush to wed too fast,
> without being really certain.
> Face enormous legal bills
> at the final curtain."

Now that we're all awake and alert again, let's visit some "questionable" places to meet singles!

Chapter Eight

QUESTIONABLE PLACES TO MEET SINGLES

Supermarkets

Dear George:

"I was shopping in a supermarket when another shopper asked me if I was single. I said I was and he asked me to dinner. I was so shocked that I told him I was already taken, even though I'm not. What should I have done?"

I think you should either change supermarkets or let the rest of the single women know where you shop.

I've heard that shopping is the coming fad in singles mingling, but I can't prove it, and I don't really have any research that shows that it is a good place to meet singles. I remember once while I was shopping in the produce department of a local supermarket, a lady came up to me and asked whether McIntoshes are good for cooking. She obviously was trying to strike up a conversation among "us singles," like she'd heard so much about. But I guess I blew it! I told her that if you cook a McIntosh, you might melt the keyboard and ruin the micro chips. She thought I was nuts! I guess some single shoppers don't have a sense of humor.

I know of a number of supermarkets that have set up singles shopping night fund-raisers, where a portion of the proceeds that night go to a charity. And I've heard through the media that many people have met and married as a result of a supermarket shopping trip, though I can't prove it.

I can see it all now. While the men are looking over the gorgeous "tomatoes" in the produce department, the women are checking out the cute "buns" in the bakery. You'll probably meet your mate in . . . where else but . . . the "meet" department.

But as I stated at the outset, the best places to meet other singles is EVERYWHERE, and supermarkets are just another example of what I mean.

It seems to me that men seem to think supermarkets are a good meeting place, more so than women. But for myself, I question that idea. Whenever I and the bachelors I know go shopping, we try to get in and out as quickly as possible. The thought of loitering around a supermarket looking for a date turns me off. But if it works for some people . . . go for it!

Here's a similar meeting place that makes more sense to me. It seems that Home Depot and Lowes specialize in more than one type of "home improvement." On one of my recent visits, I happened to notice the very large number of single men in the store. It dawned on me that this might be a good place for gals to meet single men. So I checked with a few ladies who own their own homes and they confirmed that it's a GREAT place to meet men. One lady (40's) said invariably all she needs do is look perplexed at some gadget on the shelves and at least two men will stop by and offer help. Another lady (50's) said she finds week-ends are the best days for meeting men because most work during the weekday hours.

Still another lady (49) calls Home Depot her private country club. She says in the last six months she's had at least eight men give her their business cards and ask for a dinner date. She hasn't accepted any yet but she says it's the best place she knows to meet single men. All the ladies seem to agree that the best areas to meet men were the gardening, plumbing and electrical aisles. (Now if we could only convince them to add a dance floor.)

Newspaper *"Personals"*

One female reader of my newspaper column offered to run a "personals" ad in her local newspaper to find out what a woman might expect from a lonely-hearts ad. She was 56 years young, very attractive and upbeat, and very intelligent . . . able to converse with anyone about any subject. She was a very positive person, always pleasant and smiling.

Her ad stated that she was above average in intelligence, financially and emotionally secure, and looking for a man with the same traits. She disdained the "foxy lady" approach, even though she could have qualified here too.

She received 22 replies and met with 19 of the respondents (she couldn't locate the other three). She met each of them over coffee, breakfast, or lunch in a public restaurant, and she always drove herself. Nine of the men she rejected right away as being incompatible.

The men ranged in age from 48 to 73; the average was 59 years. She talked to each man on the telephone at great length before she met him, and this gave her pretty good insight into what kind of person he'd be and whether she would meet him for a meal or just a cup of coffee. She didn't want to spend too much of her time with the ones who didn't initially sound like they were her kind of man.

The list of men she met reads like a "who's who" of dates. They included a retired college president, a radio station owner, several corporate owners and developers, school teachers, a pilot, a male model, and computer experts, and they all loved traveling and all the other interests she mentioned in her ad. She really hit the jackpot.

Four of the men ended up proposing marriage, and she dated three of them for a long time. When critiquing the respondents, she said that all were sincere and looking for a lasting relationship rather than a one-night stand. Many wanted to know how they compared to the competition, showing, she said, that men have many of the same feelings of inadequacy as women and were willing to admit it. None were bar hoppers, but all thought it was perfectly respectable to answer a dating ad.

A few, however, became openly hostile when discussing ex-wives, which seemed to put her on the spot. Her word of advice here was to tell men not to discuss their ex-wives on a date. It's boring and in bad taste, especially since the "ex" isn't around to defend herself.

This story ended up in a strange twist of fate. (Remember! Everything in this book is a true story.) This classy lady, who had so many great respondents to her to newspaper ad wanting to marry her, eventually met a man in a *lounge, of all places* and married him 5 months later.

Who says the bar scene doesn't work?

Dear George:

"I'm a 36-year-old male, 6 ft. 2 in., and considered good looking. I'm interested in finding a lady in the 25 to 35 age range. I have taken out two dating ads. I got three responses on one and four on the other, and none panned out. I also answered several ads and got next to no response. I work with my hands and only earn $28,000 a year, so I'm low on the totem pole. It seems that women have their pick of men and won't talk to anyone making less than $50,000."

This is America where you can always improve your job status with a little extra effort or education. Next time you answer an ad, don't mention your job status or salary or type of work. If you are of good character (and you sound like you are), that will end up being more important than your job. You can always change your job, but you can't change your personality. I know plenty of people who make mucho bucks but who aren't worth two cents as human beings.

Try this in a few ads you reply to and see what happens. Send your photograph (neatly dressed) and mention only your age, hobbies, interests, church affiliation, name and address. It should work!

Here's a story about mail-order dating ads that will really slay you. It's a true story; I personally verified all the facts. (Everything in this book is true, remember?)

Jim (not his real name) was a wealthy middle-aged rancher in a medium sized Midwestern town. Despite his wealth and his expensive lifestyle, he had trouble meeting women and—once he did—keeping them interested in him. He was fairly self-centered (as many millionaires are), and women found this to be a turnoff. In fact, they found it boring. With all his wealth and all the creature comforts he could offer, after nearly 10 years of searching, he was unable to find someone who would go out with him more than three or four times.

He was becoming frantic! One day, he got a "brainstorm" and wrote the following lonely hearts ad:

> Dying millionaire in 50's 6 ft. tall. Seeks a trim, attractive lady under 50 to save him from death and boredom. Send photo and details to ...

He placed this ad in the classified "personals" section of a *national* daily newspaper and received a phenomenal response. Exactly 121 women answered his ad, perhaps hoping to cash in on the largess of this "dying" millionaire. (He, of course, wasn't really ill, just dying for female companionship.) Following are some of the responses:

> One woman wrote from a penitentiary, asking him for money to buy a new RV after she was paroled. She enclosed several intimate photographs that must have been taken by her gynecologist.
>
> Another cute respondent sent him a photograph— complete with pasties in all the right places. And every month she followed up with a new photo of

herself, with more pasties in the right places. Even though he never met her personally, she must have spent a hundred bucks on her photo-of-the-month campaign.

Many of the respondents were convicts, mostly people in jail for writing bad checks. A number of women wrote to bawl him out for appealing to "fortune hunters."

A husband and wife team invited him to join them in a menage a trois. It sounded pretty sick.

A secretary wanted $8,500 for breast augmentation surgery and ended her letter saying that she would be happy to meet him in person after the operation to say "thanks for the mammaries."

Several women wanted to be "kept" and gave very graphic descriptions of their "abilities."

He received a number of letters from women in foreign countries. The farthest was from China, where a Beijing University graduate offered to be his "lady."

Many described hardships or economic problems they or their families faced and offered just about everything in exchange for a little monetary assistance.

The sad thing about this story is that some of these desperate women seemed not to understand that the man was being playful, perhaps a bit devious. It was like offering a bone to a puppy dog and pulling it away just as he goes for it.

The world of mail-order dating can be a strange world, populated by some strange people.

I'm not a big fan of mail-order dating ads. You might be surprised that I have these feelings after reading a few of the success stores, which show that these ads can really draw attention. . .and results.

My feelings about this type of singles activity stems from an experience I once had in a lounge. A woman joined two men sitting next to me and pulled out a large envelope stuffed with replies to a "personals" ad she had run in a local newspaper. She and the two men proceeded to open and read aloud the dozen or so letters she received, to the amusement of everyone else around the bar. They made fun of the respondents, even to the point of mentioning their names. What was meant to be a private letter by the writer was being shared with everyone at the bar.

When you answer a dating ad in writing you never know the type of person who placed it.

Nudist Resorts

Dear George:

"What do you know about nudist camps, as far as their being good places to meet other singles?"

I guess it depends on how THOROUGHLY you want to meet them. I do know several prominent businessmen who married as a result of meeting their mates in a nudist resort. But, from what I understand, it is very difficult for a single person to even get in to these resorts. For one thing, most want to avoid hanky-panky, and they try to keep the ratio of men to women even. Furthermore, they try to be more family oriented, from what I hear.

I heard of one nudist camp that had marble slabs for benches. Whenever people sat down it sounded like someone applauding.

I once ran a list of goofy questions in my newspaper column addressed to nudists. As far as sitting on marble slabs, I was politely informed that all nudists carry a towel with them and always sit on this towel (okay, so it sounds like people applauding with their gloves on). Here are some of the other questions and answers I received:

Where do nudists keep their loose change, keys, and so on, since they don't have pockets? A man answered that they carry such items in a little "hanging pouch." (Now my next question is, where does he hang the pouch? Don't answer that!)

What do they do if they don't like volleyball? Do they allow touch football, or is that illegal? One woman replied that it's more fun WATCHING volleyball than playing it. Another said they have all the sports you'd expect to find in any high-class resort. (Oh yeah? I'll bet they don't have ice skating!)

Are they allowed to place a napkin on their laps at mealtime, or is that cheating? Respondents indicated that many nudists dress up for dinner . . . and then undress for dessert.

Is it polite to stare? Not anymore than it is at any other place, I was told.

Are there rules against crossing your legs? No.

When you are introduced to a lady, do you compliment her on her hairdo or what? I was told you should give her a compliment just like you would someone with clothes on. It seems to me you'd be insulting the lady if you complimented her on her hairdo, since you obviously would be looking at the wrong place.

When you bump into someone, do you say excuse me or thank you? There were no answers to this one, so I suspect you say thank you.

When I ran this article on nudists, I never realized there were so many "closet" nudists in all sorts of occupations. They all seemed to be pretty good sports, and none of them got mad at me for all the puns I made at their expense. I have to take my hat off to them. (But that's ALL I'll take off!)

Some modern-day nudist resorts have condominiums on the premises, where residents live year-round. Most resorts are oriented toward families and strictly supervise the people who attend. Many allow first-time visitors to attend with their clothes on to see whether they like it. I understand that most visitors quickly shed their duds once they see everyone else doing it and, subsequently, hardly pay any attention to the nudity.

An amusing note: First-time guests to a nudist camp are referred to as "bunnies," a reference to their unmistakably pink rear ends.

But as far as singles meeting other singles, my guess is you could better spend your time elsewhere.

But, I finally did it! After writing jokes about it for years, I took the plunge. I visited a nudist colony. I wanted to check out for myself if this was a good place for singles to meet other singles. (Oh! The sacrifices I make for you dear readers!)

To say it was shocking is putting it mildly. But, like most things, once I got used it, it seemed very normal. No one seemed to stare at others, only me. It was a little discomforting and I didn't know whether to be proud or embarrassed.

I visited with a friend who had a membership there, but even though he was a member, it was very difficult for two men to get past the front gate. They restrict admission to couples only so they don't have a bunch of leering bachelors ogling all their female members. Afer I swore on a stack of discarded clothing that we wouldn't ogle and leer, they very reluctantly let me pay the $25 fee and enter. This hassle indicated right away to me that these places are no place to meet other singles, since they only want couples. So write it off your list.

Wow! What a sight! It's billed as a clothing optional resort but no one had a stitch on. After you park your car, you leave your clothes in the car and walk into the compound (I never did ask where they all kept their car keys, darn it!) It was a hot day and the place was jammed with 3,000 people, all in Birthday suits. And no one seemed to notice it or care about it . . . except those who were staring at *me*!

Everyone seemed proud of themselves and happy with themselves no matter what size or shape they were, and I guess that's good! They have a mini-shopping mall, plus a restaurant and several bars grouped around their swimming pools. I visited their clothing boutique expecting it to be empty but was surprised to learn that they sell more clothing than anything else in the resort. But I still couldn't avoid it . . . the sales clerks staring at *me*, smilingly!

They have a hotel ($54 a night) , a lot of condominiums (people live there year-round), a lake and all sorts of sports activities including the stereotypical volleyball courts. I took a golf cart tour of the entire area and saw condo owners washing their cars in their driveways, wives hanging laundry out to dry, neighbors chatting over the back fence. Just like any small town, except all were naked as jay birds. And they all seemed to stare at *me* as we drove by.

Luckily there was a football game on TV that day, so I was able to watch it at their bar and give my eyes a rest. (Ogling and leering can become tiresome after a while). But even the bartenders stared at *me*!

With 3,000 bare bodies crammed-in "cheek to jowl" all over the place, I couldn't help wonder who owns the sun tan lotion concession. He must be a jillionaire!

When the sun began to set and the air began to cool, it was time to return to the land of clothing before this place turned into goose-bump city. As I departed the resort, it suddenly dawned on me why everyone kept staring at me: I was the only one in the whole place wearing SHORTS!

Professional Match-Making Services

One of my singles column readers gave me some information about the real costs of joining a popular nationally recognized singles dating service. The one he told me about advertises their service quite extensively on television and is probably one of the better-known services around the country. They advertise a "come-on" price in their ads, but I don't think you can rely on these prices.

They'll usually have two or more packages to sell. Of the two they'll usually discuss, one guarantees that you'll meet at least 3 people a month (36 a year), for a yearly enrollment fee of nearly a thousand dollars. This comes out to about $30 per introduction.

The other package guarantees that you'll meet at least one new person a month for 9 months, (hmmm, I wonder why 9 months?), giving you a total of nine new acquaintances for a fee of a little over $400. This comes to nearly $50 per introduction.

And, of course, there's always a "catch." The catch here is that the dates you are introduced to may live as far away as 50 miles. That's a heck of a long trip for a blind date, as far as I'm concerned.

I've got a great idea! Instead of spending this $400 for nine blind dates, I think it would be better if you took 80 five-dollar bills (totaling $400), wrote your name and phone number in the margin of each bill, and stood on the street corner and passed them out to everyone who looked pretty or handsome. At least you would know that anyone who bites is at least an attractive date and that they're from your locale. I think you might actually get quite a few people responding. Anyway, it's just an idea.

One lady said she paid $5,000 cash for an 18 month membership in a nationally known dating service. She specified what type of man she was seeking (Ht., wt., age, education) but got introduced to anything but what she wanted. However, the fine print in her contract stated that as long as she got a "referral," they had a "no refund policy." She got stuck with her loss and they refused a refund—even though she never met one man even close to what she was seeking.

Another man said he paid $1,000 to join a similar dating service. (The men always get in cheaper—sometimes for free! How's THAT for sex discrimination?) Even at his "bargain" price they weren't able to introduce him to any compatible women.

Another described the sales pitch they use to sign up lonely widows and other women. They probe to find her weak points and then work on them. He said: "If they *cry*, they *buy*!" How's THAT for being cold-blooded? Really disgusting!

Usually, more women than men enroll in these matchmaking services, and they usually have a devil of a time trying to find enough men to go around. Dating services are sort of like employment agencies: if they send you around to enough potential employers (or potential dates in this case), one of them might stick. But the odds are that after you've spent a year with a dating service, you will have been rejected so many times by so many prospective dates that your self-esteem may become shattered.

I remember receiving a questionnaire from a "highly respected" dating service. It had about fifty questions relating to my background, needs, and desires. My answers were to be fed into a computer and *viola*, the printout would list my perfect mate, including her name, address and phone number.

I contacted a lady friend of mine who had also received the same questionnaire in the mail. We each agreed to fill in identical answers for all the questions. Surely the computer would quickly match us up. Even a child of 10, when comparing our answers—our likes and dislikes, our wants and desires—would immediately surmise that we were truly made for each other . . . a match made in heaven.

Not so! This dating service had other plans for me. They wanted to spread this male around to keep as many women happy as possible . . . and keep them enrolled in the service. Then, perhaps, after I had burned myself out squiring all their conscripts, they would find my perfect match, my lady friend with the identical questionnaire, and we'd live happily ever after (and we'd be expected to state this in their testimonial ads, you can be sure).

I think you can save all the money you'd spend on these dating services if you follow the tips in this book. (And feel free to mail me a check for the amount of money you saved!)

My research shows that a lot of these match-making services don't last very long, probably because they are competing with all the low-cost and no-cost methods, so they all need a special "gimmick." It seems the latest "gimmick" is where they set you up for a Dutch

Treat meal or cocktails with a blind date at an upscale restaurant or lounge. They charge a membership fee of between $1,000 and $2,000 a year and—like other dating services, they personally interview you to see if you qualify. If you've got the entrance fee, chances are you qualify.

Television *"Phone-A-Date"* Scams

Being a glutton for punishment (and to include as many examples as I could in this book), I tried another dating service advertised on television that said I could meet the woman of my dreams. The commercial showed dozens of skimpily clad women in all sorts of beckoning positions, and superimposed over them was the message "FREE CALL" !!

I had to try it. So I called the FREE telephone number on the screen. A sexy-sounding woman welcomed me to her lair and said I could talk to their gorgeous models if I called—guess what—a "900" number! She told me if I called this number now, I'd be connected to the Caribbean island where the orgy was being held. So I got sucked-in and dialed the number, having been forewarned that it would cost me $3.99 a minute and that I must be over 18 years of age.

The first voice that came on the phone wasted a lot of my valuable (and costly) time by explaining that I could talk to the woman of my choice by pressing "1" for the orgy room or "2" for the "hot box." Since it was a chilly evening, I pressed "2" for the hot box. A sensuous sounding woman came on the line, welcomed me to the hot box, and listed a few women's names I could date over the phone. I chose to talk to Dominique, the first name she gave me. After a lot of beeping and squeaking and static (at $3.99 per minute), a voice came on and said that there were 146 callers ahead of me waiting to talk to Dominique, and that if I didn't want to hang on until she was free, I could talk to another woman on the list. So I selected Donna, and again, after all the costly beeps and static, I was informed that Donna had six callers ahead of me and that I could wait or press a button for another lady. I pressed another button and was told my "date" Terry had four callers ahead of me, and so on. I hung up before my phone bill equaled the national debt. I'm willing to bet that there were NO WOMEN available to talk to me or anyone else. They just took advantage of us gullible men and pocketed a sheer profit of $40. I guess I've proven beyond any doubt that calling "900" numbers to meet a woman is the absolute DUMBEST way to meet other singles!

Reading The Obituaries

More and more women are using the obituary columns of their local newspaper to find their mate. They know that many widowers have a tendency to latch on to the first friendly face that comes along and they try to make sure they are that first "friendly face." One widower told me that more than a dozen women—all strangers— called him after his wife's funeral, inviting him to dinner. It seems that these women read the obituary pages and when they see there is a male survivor somewhere around the age group they are seeking, they set up a campaign to nail him. They wait a respectable time— like 2 days after the funeral—and then spring their traps.

That same widower encountered women who even attended the wakes to meet or look over the surviving male, posing as friends of the deceased wife (who, by the way, isn't around to dispute that friendship). The next thing you know, we'll have to fight off these "widower spiders" at the deathbeds of sick wives.

But they all seem to know what they're doing, because in many cases, the new widower is easily led down the primrose path to the altar. It is my observation that nearly half of newly widowed men are putty in the hands of aggressive females and, not knowing what to do in the situation, follow her dictates. And in most cases, their lives with the new aggressive females who snagged them are more like a prison sentence.

But hold it! Before the male readers begin to feel smug about themselves, here's what a *female funeral director* told me about men (usually widowers) after she read my newspaper column on this "wake-shopping" subject. She says that men will attend the wakes of deceased husbands and tell the widow they know how she feels (since he supposedly recently experienced the same) and invite her to dinner. And some men are even more macabre, according to this source. Men will cruise through cemeteries and if they see a woman placing flowers on a gravesite, they'll stop and try to determine if she is a grieving widow. If she is: Bingo! He hits on her! (I guess that will wipe-off the "smug look" on any male readers' faces).

Chapter Nine

KEEP YOUR EYES WIDE OPEN

No matter where you go and who you meet, it's always best to be somewhat cautious before you jump into a friendship or relationship with both feet. Get to know the person better. And while this book is founded on POSITIVE THINKING, TRUST, SOCIABILITY, FRIENDSHIP & COMRADERY, every so often, we have to "fess up" to real life in the real world: everyone isn't as perfect as we should like them to be. Here are some examples:

A few readers said they had experienced some ugly possessiveness problems with their dates, and they wondered how pervasive is this problem with other couples? So I did my usual research among men and women, and came up with some real "eye-openers" as far as jealousy and possessiveness are concerned.

Some of these examples are so incredible that you might think I made them up! But swear to God they're all true. I personally checked them out.

- One man was so possessive and jealous of his girlfriend that he removed the wheels from her car so she'd have to stay home. Incredible!
- Another incredibly possessive creep took the house keys from his girlfriend because he knew she wouldn't leave her home unlocked.
- One guy made possessiveness a family affair. He had his father and sister check on his girlfriend while he was at work.
- One man helped a lady friend move some furniture and now she thinks she owns him. She continually butts in if he talks to another woman—or dances with one—even though he did

nothing but be a good neighbor. I heard the same story from another man who did a plumbing favor for a woman. These gals suddenly decided they "own" the guys and became a big nuisance. The men now are hesitant about doing favors for other women, fearing they'll get the same reaction.

- One jealous male put a phone block on their telephone so his girlfriend couldn't call her out-of-area relatives. One man (remember, these are true stories) made his bride agree (in writing) that she would not speak to any other man without his prior approval. And she was stupid enough to agree to this medieval requirement. Naturally, under these appalling conditions, the marriage didn't last very long.

Many times a man will buy a few drinks for a lady, or even do some "moonlight necking" with her, and now she thinks she belongs at the top of his dating list and if he dates someone else, she gets her nose out of joint and won't speak to him anymore. We all have experienced this a dozen times at least. Single people have to realize a good time and a great date don't signify "ownership" of the other person. "A KISS IS NOT A CONTRACT."

I personally know of quite a few potentially great relationships that were ruined by this sudden demanding of ownership of the other person.

But, getting back to creeps:

- One woman was allowed to spend exactly 30 minutes on her weekly grocery shopping. Anything longer and he suspected her of cheating on him.
- Another man was jealous of his girlfriend's relationship *with her own children* from a previous marriage. You can't beat THAT for insecurity!
- One gal said that if she dressed nicely when they went out, her boyfriend accused her of "dressing for other men." It seems a lot of men want their girlfriends to dress conservatively—

even drably—so they won't attract the attention of other men. (No. This is not in IRAN, it's in the U.S.A.)

- One lady worked late hours and whenever she arrived home her boyfriend would be standing in the driveway in his bathrobe, looking at his wristwatch. . . as if she luckily "just made it home on time!"

Here's another popular problem: Often a couple will enjoy two or three dates and have a great time. But if he or she doesn't profess their total undying love by this time, the other person becomes perturbed and shuts off any further dating. It happens all the time!

Jealousy and possessiveness are the biggest causes of relationship break-ups. So how can we overcome this destructive tendency? Here are a few ideas:

1. Resolve that neither of you owns the other one. (Slavery is a thing of the past!)
2. Appreciate the great times you have with your date-and do it with no strings attached.
3. Make yourself so attractive and charming and desirable to your date that he/she will voluntarily *wish to become your possession.* And leave it at that.

If you spot a jealousy trend from the start, stop the relationship right now. He/she will only get worse. Most of the jealous people in my research were also unfaithful to their boy/girl friends. Probably their guilty consciences caused them to mistrust others.

Are you ready for a few more examples of people who DIDN'T REALLY KNOW their partner? Remember! These are all true! I personally checked them out!

One man I met—a very successful businessman, age 45, attractive, athletic, faithfully married to his wife of 16 years. He planned to remain married to her for the rest of his life and provided her with all the love and creature comforts she could ever want.

Early one morning, she woke him up and shocked him with: "Wake up honey. The movers will be here in five minutes." It so happened she had hired movers to take all their furnishings to a new home she had rented on the sly, to live with her new boyfriend of one month. The husband hadn't the slightest inkling she was cheating on him. It came like a bolt out of the blue. Even her own family was stunned at her decision to leave this perfect marriage.

In the divorce proceedings, naturally, she wanted the lion's share of their considerable assets so she can keep her new (much younger) boyfriend in the manner to which he would like to become accustomed. To add insult to injury, the husband had been recovering from a year-long bout with cancer and was now in remission. Boy! What timing! For gals like this they should change the wedding vows. Instead of "Til death do us part" it should be "Until younger stud comes along do us part!"

Here's an even worse example of a man going into a relationship with his eyes firmly SHUT! This widower - Don - met this lovely woman - Georgina. She had a great sense of humor (he said) and they began a six year relationship. He didn't even notice how insanely jealous and possessive she was. But she had a good reason: She didn't want to lose this "meal ticket" he represented. For example, he had her house repaired and repainted, he refurnished the whole house with furnishings of her choice, bought an expensive new outdoor shed to replace the eyesore she had in her yard, remodeled many of her interior rooms and paid for all the landscaping around her home. To top it all off, he even took her on three ocean-going cruises and a number of trips to Vegas. No wonder she didn't want to lose him . . . yet!

But one day—as he tells it—they were together on a bleak, rainy Saturday with nothing to do so he suggested that they go to the mall and buy whatever else she needed around her home. She said she couldn't think of anything else she needed; he had already bought her everything. So he jokingly said: "Well I guess you don't need me anymore."

Little did he know how prophetic this comment was. She dropped him the following weekend like a hot potato, using the excuse that she didn't like him to be calling a 93 year old bedridden widow as he had been. (He'd call this woman to keep her spirits up and wish her happy Mother's Day, Merry Christmas, and check on her health. He'd do it about 6 times a year, all via telephone.)

How do you like this story for the ultimate in *insanity*? But not just for the insanely jealous and possessive woman, but also for the naivete of the man who purposely led himself to the slaughter. (As I mentioned previously, this is a true story that I thoroughly checked out). An even sadder note is that this 93 year old widow that he occasionally called to keep her spirits up, passed away two months later.

May she rest in peace.

Here's another example of people we should avoid like the plague.

I was sitting in this crowded upscale lounge recently and noticed an older man sitting at the end of the bar, next to an empty seat. After a while, two pleasant ladies entered, one sat in the empty seat and the other stood behind her, and they ordered their beverages. As soon as they received—*and paid for*—their beverages, this guy struck up a conversation with both women. I sort of eavesdropped because I wondered if he was ever going to be gentleman enough to offer the standing lady his seat.

But even more shocking was his conversation. He "interviewed" these ladies about their financial situations because, as he said he was looking for a woman to support him and he was pre-qualifying these ladies. He was dead serious! The women—between exchanging strange glances at each other—pretty much humored him. They certainly were more polite than they should have been. After about a half hour of this financial interview, the guy offered his seat to the standing lady, saying "I don't offer my seat to just anyone!" What a creep! Whoever told him he was God's gift to women sure led him astray. To make it worse, he looked like late 60's and the gals mid-50's. And he was dressed like a slob!

Whenever you ladies encounter a totally self-centered oaf like this, I give you permission to utter my copyrighted, patented and registered phrase which is: *BUG OFF YOU CREEP!* Feel free to use it as often as necessary.

But, just to prove that this book is an "equal opportunity" book, I might caution the men to beware of overly-aggressive women who believe they have been betrayed. . . like Lorena Bobbitt.

I talked to one man who had a big fight with his brand new wife in the limousine—on his way from church to his wedding reception. That marriage ended 10 months later. Or how about a world renowned astrologist who should have known better and married the town's obnoxious drunkard? That lasted only 2 days. Now you know the importance of "Keeping Your Eyes Open."

Chapter Ten

UNDERSTANDING OTHER SINGLES

Dear George:

"I've entered a new phase in my life. I finally feel like a seasoned single person. I have felt desired, rejected, superior, inferior, confident, uncomfortable, lonely, happy to be alone, restless, and peaceful. I have learned to come out of the married shell. I am more conscious of my appearance and conversation. I am less domestic, more artistic and creative. I feel braver. I can handle tasks easier. I make my own decisions. I am more assertive, and sometimes it makes me appear a bit selfish and self-centered. There is excitement in the air . . .adventure awaits me."

"I am now a grown-up SINGLE WOMAN!"

What a nice way to start a hard-to-write chapter about understanding singles.

However, here's a letter from another woman who seems less optimistic. She's 48 years old and widowed: "I know one thing for sure. It's tough being single these days. Times have changed and dating seems almost obsolete; the kind of date where dinner and a movie or dancing afterward takes place. That seems to be reserved for those who are already involved in a relationship, or married. I asked a girlfriend the other day when was the last time she went on a date like I described. Her reply: I can't remember when, it's been so long. Just my thinking exactly.

"One thing that I know has changed since say the 80's; women used to get together and talk about their latest dates and always the first questions asked were What does he do for a living?, Does he drive a nice car?, Does he have a house?, Is he secure financially?

"Now it's the men who are asking those questions as much as women. It's as though you have to be financially compatible to even get a date because you know at some point he may want to introduce you to friends or family and those questions are going to be asked. You do not want to appear less than your friends and, oh no! Do not dissatisfy the family.

"One of my lady friends in her early fifties said it best the other day. She dates a gentleman every now and then in his early sixties. He said to her: Why don't we get married? You have more money than any woman I know. I'm sure he meant it as a joke, sort of. But part of that stings because it's true. My friend is secure financially and that part of her is very attractive to men.

"But what happens to the single person who just plain works for a living? They very often are overlooked because they have nothing to bring to the table, so to speak, besides a not-so-new car, a minor bank account and maybe a rental property or a mortgage or something small. Not very attractive to men.

"There are plenty of really good average people out there. I believe society is just making it really difficult for us to date or even find a date because we can't get past these questions. And times have changed. The answers matter!"

Knowing how and what people think is the first important step to understanding singles, but we have to be good listeners in order to do this. Having conducted so many research interviews over the years, I have had to become a *good listener* or I wouldn't have enough material to fill a column. Maybe it would be a good idea if we all pretended that we were writing a singles column. . .we'd hang on every word the other person is saying. We'd become good listeners.

Here are a few examples of how being a good listener gave me insight into understanding singles better: I was talking to a gorgeous lady (early 50's) who was telling me about the time a few years ago when she was LOVESICK and I found it hard to believe. Her boyfriend lived with her *in her home* but still he screamed and yelled at her so much that even the neighbors complained about the noise.

He would constantly put her down, call her names and insult her in front of others, yet she still put up with the jerk. . . for 5 *long years*! She explains that she was in love with him and kept hoping he would change. He never did!

I wanted to see if this was an isolated case so I checked out a few other women. One woman totally supported her boyfriend and paid all his expenses even though he would occasionally beat her up. She is a gorgeous blonde and he is a total leech, but she was LOVE SICK and supported him for over 4 years—and through dozens of beatings—until she received one beating too many and woke up!

Another lady told me about the ultra-possessive relationship she was in with a boyfriend. She wasn't allowed to leave the house or phone anyone unless he was with her! Incredible! She also admits to being LOVESICK and after 6 years, snapped out of it and escaped HER OWN HOME by climbing over the backyard fence and running away.

And we all read the newspapers where a man is accused of allegedly raping a mother and her 14-year-old daughter, but the mother still loves him and visits him in jail and sends him love letters. Unbelievable!

It seems to me that ALL of the parties in all of these cases need to see a good shrink pronto! Maybe some people who are in an abusive relationship, after reading this might snap out of it and get their lives back on track. I hope so!

Speaking of shrinks, like anything else there are good and bad psychiatrists and psychologists. It's pretty easy to call yourself a marriage counselor or a personal counselor these days. (I counted 133 in my phone directory). But you should check them out as thoroughly as you would a heart surgeon or a brain surgeon. They should have a University degree in their specialty field. They should be successful (ask for references). And they should possess an open mind—not like the case I heard of where a female counselor hates all men and this unfairness shows up in her advice to other women. I don't think this hateful attitude helps patients. I think it ruins them.

Or another case where a marriage counselor has been divorced THREE times. How can he tell me how to save my one marriage when he couldn't save his three marriages? Give me a break!

Some people who have simply had a lovers spat will rush to seek counseling when maybe all they needed was loyalty, humility and the ability to forgive.

Of course, some people are impossible to understand.

I once received a letter from a woman in her late 30's who happened to live in my same city. She was new to the area and wrote that she couldn't get up enough nerve to attend any of the numerous singles events that were going on, even though there was a wide variety of functions to choose from. She also mentioned that she didn't have a job, and was at a loss as to where to start looking, and would appreciate any help I could give her.

I called her on the telephone soon after receiving her letter and suggested that we meet and put our heads together to help work out a solution for her and get her off to a flying start in her new city. She readily agreed to it, and we scheduled a meeting for 1:00 p.m. the following day at a public place that she suggested. I gave her a phone number to call in case she had a change of plans.

Then, on my own, without her knowledge, I invited two of the area's most eligible bachelors to join us after 1:30 p.m., sort of as a surprise encounter. One of the men had a few job openings in his business and said that he would be happy to discuss them with her. I thought it would be a friendly gesture and make her feel more welcome to the city. Also, it would give her the opportunity to get to know three bachelors who were all gentlemen and thoroughly above-board. Then, if she ever did decide to attend a singles function in the future, she would at least know us, since we all attended most of them, and we could help introduce her to other people with interests similar to hers.

In addition, as an extra benefit, she might qualify for employment from one of my friends, if her job credentials met his job requirements. It felt good knowing that I'd helped someone I hadn't even met. I was sure it would be a pleasant afternoon.

So guess what happened?

I showed up on time! My two bachelor friends showed up on time! BUT SHE NEVER SHOWED UP! Nor did she call the number I gave her. Many years have gone by since this incident, and I still haven't received a letter or an excuse or an apology or anything from her. I guess I can conclude that I was just plain stood up! And so were my two bachelor friends, who, by the way will never do this favor for me again.

The thing that bugs me the most is that I went out of my way to be a good friend to someone I'd never seen or met, and I got left holding the bag—not even a phone call or short note. I can't believe it!

Here's a letter from a single man that helps us better understand a male's thinking, for all you new widowers:

"After three years of being single, I know this is not the way I want to spend the rest of my life . . . alone. I'm sure there are plenty of singles that feel the same way and yet we all seem to have our "excuses" as to why we're still alone.

"Trying to find that special someone is not an easy quest! I think we try too hard sometimes and become disappointed in ourselves and others. This is the hard part to understand: we need to lighten up and learn not to take ourselves so seriously. How we meet that person that makes us feel that feeling once again, is so many times by accident. Tell that person who lights up your life how you feel about them. The worst that can happen is that a person says thank you but I'm involved with someone. You've still made them feel great and you should also! You have just expressed yourself to another human being, someone that attracted you and that's got to feel good. We

don't give ourselves enough credit for trying. It's not easy, but as they say, nothing tried, nothing gained.

"Keep your eyes open at any kind of function you enjoy: out-door markets, art shows, museums, concerts, libraries and book stores, the beach and marinas; you get the idea. These are going to be the people that have the same interests as you, so get out there and look and talk!

"The bottom line is you have to make an effort; both men and women, to let your feelings be known. Who knows! someone could end up your friend, your lover and companion to share your life with!"

Here's one thing I could never understand about women: when two women get together in a restaurant, in a lounge, at a dance or a party, or ANYWHERE for that matter, WHAT DO YOU FIND TO TALK ABOUT ALL THE TIME? Whenever I see two women together, they are ALWAYS totally engrossed in conversation with each other, even though they may have been together all day or all week! Don't you gals ever run out of things to talk about? You always appear interested and excited about your conversations and never look bored! After hours and hours of chatting, what's left to say?

I know when two MEN get together under similar circumstances, we run out of things to say in about 5 minutes or so.

I asked a lovely lady what she and her girlfriends talk about so much! I finally pinned her down, The topics of their conversations include discussing old and new friends, and trashing a few of them, situations at work and at home, clothes and stupid outfits worn by others, guys who are cute, dance combos they like and dislike, things they like and dislike about men, ways for women to rule the world, and animal rights. And if they're in a lounge that offers dancing, "girl talk" allows them to appear more interested in their conversation than in the men around them and, thus, less like an easy "pick up."

If she's the average woman, we men now at least have a clue about how to break up these "matched sets" and start a conversation of our own with one of them. Here's an idea: approach one of the women whom you find attractive and bet her a dance that you can name one of the subjects that she and her friends have been discussing all evening long. She'll probably accept your challenge, so then tell her one of the subjects listed in the previous paragraph. If she's honest and admits it, you've got yourself a dancing partner. And if she denies they talked about any of these subjects, so what? Ask her for the dance anyhow! You've broken the ice, and that's what they're really there for in the first place.

This lady told me so!

Dear George:

"You told women not to give out their phone numbers and addresses to new acquaintances, and now that's messing it up for us men. They're using you as their reason for not giving them out."

Hooray! Let's face it: Women are becoming more clever and more careful. They're only giving out pertinent information to those they know and trust. That's the way it should be, what with all the creeps on the loose these days. It's the only safe way to go, and you should respect them for it.

Did it ever dawn on you that maybe these women really don't want you to call them and they're just using me as an excuse?

Dear George:

"Why don't you tell your female readers that men don't like possessive women?"

One of the biggest complaints in the singles world—and I've heard it from men by the score—is that some women, and men too, tend to become possessive after two or three dates, sometimes after one date!

It's worth repeating that possessiveness wrecks more potential relationships than any other single factor, in my book. Sometimes a man or woman seems to think that because they had a good time together, and maybe whispered sweet nothings in each other's ear, that he is HERS or she is HIS. I've heard that some singles even start to make plans for the other's weekend activities or begin to expect him or her to *account for time* spent apart. Many think they shouldn't date others. In short, they suddenly "own" the other person.

This possessiveness is a single person's greatest fear, and it automatically triggers a defensive reaction in which they subconsciously overly assert their independence, and the whole relationship goes down the tubes.

The only time you really can think that you OWN the guy or gal is when you're both standing before a preacher and you've got a "you-know-what" license in your hip pocket. And even then, don't take this ownership for granted.

Dear George:

"I've gone with a girl for 7 months. I take her to dinner, dancing, sports, etc., and we have a very good time together. However, when I take her home, she suddenly becomes as cold as an ice cube. I've always treated her as a gentleman should, and maybe that's my problem."

I think SHE has the problem, not you. Some people are "givers" and some are "takers." Sounds to me like you've got a real "taker," and she seems to be taking YOU for granted. Life is too short. Move on!

And continue to be a gentleman. Most women appreciate it.

Here are two letters I received—one from a woman and the other from a man—that show how maladjusted some people can become out there in singles-land. Both of the writers seem to me totally into themselves, and such people usually can only get "losers" for dates. As far as I'm concerned, they got what they deserved. Read on!

Dear George:

"I was married for 30 years (true blue). Suddenly, my husband left me for a much younger woman. I am an attractive, intelligent, outgoing woman. Seeking friendly companionship, I decided to try some singles social events. What a put-down! I found (probably the result of the ratio of single men to women) that the 50 to 60 year old men at each event gravitated to the 35 to 45 year old women, leaving us 45 to 55 year olds sitting like undiscovered wallflowers.

"When I was finally asked to dance at one event, I was held in a body lock suitable for points in any wrestling match. Moreover, when I pulled back, I was called a cold fish by possibly the rudest man I've ever met. Having just begun, I quit!

"I'll stay home before I'll subject myself to such demeaning treatment again. I'm not as desperate as all those pot-stomached, hair-receding Romeos seem to think all us gals sitting on the sidelines are.

"Some of us—I dare say many—are modest, caring, respectable mothers and grandmothers who would much rather be home making popcorn and watching old movies on TV but for some reason or other have found ourselves seeking the company of others. Personally, I think many of you (50-ish) fellas are missing the boat. We (50-ish) women are not after your money (we have our own). We don't need your security (we are secure). You don't have to dress and act like you are 30-ish (we like 50-ish). We understand going to bed early (for rest). Now if by chance, after reading this, some of you men decide to ask us to dance, please remember you are probably holding someone's mother in your arms.

"Show a little respect.

Just had to blow off some steam. Thanks for listening."

Whew!!! There's more!

Dear George:

"I've had it with modern-day single women. I have never met more rude, inconsiderate women in my life. Of the four women I *recently made dates with, one stood me up cold, no explanation, nothing! One broke four dates in a row, including dinner and theater, with tickets in hand. One broke two out of three dates (left a message 3 hours prior to date time on my answering machine). One left a message on my answering machine 2 hours before our date saying, "Something came up!" All this was in a 30-day period. The broken dates were not just simple "find something to do" evenings. I had made many preparations.*

"I started asking myself, "What's the matter with you? Ugly? Masher? Womanizer?"

My friends say I'm a nice guy and that I have class, money, looks, and respect for women.

"If a woman isn't sure she can be there, she shouldn't make a date. If a true emergency comes up that causes her to break a date, she shouldn't rely on a cold answering machine to relay the reason. She should personally tell her date the reason. To the women who wonder why some men take you out, get what they want, and dump you, they probably were at one time a nice guy like me who got tired of being shoved around."

Boy, what a lot of garbage! It seems to me we're sinking into the sea of ego trips and self-pity with these two people. It's too bad they're from different cities; they sound like they'd make an excellent pair. I can see them on a date now, sitting alone on a moonlit night, complaining about how bad everyone else is (except themselves, of course). Both of these writers are being grossly unfair by condemning all singles for the actions of a few. I hear this same junk 20 times a day.

I know of a thousand great singles for every jerk—male and female. And speaking for the pot-stomached, hair-receding men among us, I object to the woman's discriminating description.

Many of us male singles are FATHERS who deserve the same respect she claims she deserves as a mother. Her bitterness toward men is obvious, probably brought to a head as a result of her husband leaving her for another woman (or did he escape?). She seems to forget it was HIS action, not ours. Give the rest of us a break, lady, and back off!

As far as the self-pitying male on his own ego trip, I agree that anyone who stands up another person is lower than a worm's kneecaps. But he had *seven* dates in 1 month that were canceled by the gals. In this day and age, when we have such a large plurality of single women over single men, he set a world's record for canceled dates. I don't think he should waste his time wondering what's wrong with women. I think he should instead worry about what's wrong with HIM.

However, things always work out for the better. He can spend the money he saved from these seven canceled dates on a good shrink. It might be the best investment he'll ever make.

And while he's at it, he should get rid of that telephone answering machine. Maybe he'll get more dates if they can't cancel them.

Dear George:

"I was married for 25 years and am now divorced. I am 45 years old, love to dance, and adore men. I have gone to several singles dances and happy hours. My problem is that for some reason it seems the only men interested in me are in their 60's. They are very nice, but I don't feel comfortable with the age difference, and I would much prefer meeting someone my own age.

"It seems the men my age are only interested in "pretty young things." By the way, even though I'm a mother, I love to be held close while dancing. The gal who wrote you that letter can stay home in front of the TV by herself."

Obviously, this letter was written in response to the letter printed on the preceding pages (by the woman who was put into a wrestling body lock while dancing). The nice thing about this newspaper business is that when we get depressed by an extremely negative letter writer, we get picked right back up again by nice, positive thinking, lovely people.

Now if we can only figure out a way for this letter writer to be noticed at parties by 45-year-old men . . . hmmmmm!

Lady! How are you at handstands?

Dear George:

"Why do most single and married men expect the woman to do the laundry and cleaning, even when she is working full-time also?"

Let's look at it from a husband/wife angle, just for a breather. You mentioned the old female complaint of having to do the laundry. If you have to take your wash to the Laundromat, then I agree it's an inconvenience. And if you have to beat your clothes clean with rocks on the bank of a stream, then it's definitely a hassle. But the gals I have heard complain the most about doing laundry have an automatic washer and dryer. What's the big deal?

In my married days, I was led to believe laundry was a horrible chore. But now that I've done my own laundry for more than a dozen years, I've found it's really no big deal.

First you toss the clothes into the washer (along with assorted loose change, a wallet or two, and a Bic that soon won't flick anymore) and wait for the buzzer to sound. Then you toss the whole mess into the dryer and wait for another buzzer. Big deal! Total actual work time involved—3 minutes. And since all the clothes are wash and wear you simply stuff them into drawers and viola! The whole chore is completed.

Now about the other complaint about cleaning the house. Usually the male partner cuts the grass and cares for the exterior of the house and does all the manual, menial labor inside and out. I'll bet by the end of the year, if you add up how much time each one spends doing their particular chores, you'll both end up in a dead heat, 50-50. (O.K., Men! I think I got us off the hook!)

Speaking of married people; did you ever notice how married women tend to treat us singles as though we have leprosy or something? I once attended a planning meeting where married and single women were planning a local charitable event. It was very noticeable that most of the married women were just "putting up with" the single women, as if their ideas and opinions weren't really worth listening to. It was so obvious that it was disgusting. I couldn't help but chuckle, however, knowing that in a couple of years the odds are that probably a third of these snobbish women will have joined the ranks of us singles.

Revenge will be sweet!

Dear George:

"I would like to know why there are so many married men out there who don't bother to wear wedding bands. I've heard all the arguments, and none of them wash. Most of us single women can tell a married man with or without a wedding ring. Though we do get fooled occasionally, most of us would not go out with a married man by choice. So when it happens, we're as shocked as anyone. Tell your married and engaged female readers not to blame the "other" woman but to blame themselves and their husbands when something like this happens."

Sounds to me like you've just been hoodwinked by a married man posing as a single. Sorry about that! We single men have enough problems finding good, single women. We don't need any more competition.

You can usually spot the married men by the band of pure white skin on their ring finger, where their wedding ring normally is, or by the Band-Aid they wear on this finger to cover up the white band of skin.

You can also detect them very easily because they are the ones who need to "score" right away. They know they don't have much time before their spouses hunt them down and give them hell.

Single men, on the other hand, have all night . . . so to speak!

Here's another thing that mystifies me about some single

women: The number of them who seek out MARRIED MEN for their liaisons. I've talked to some single women who date ONLY married men. I asked one once why she would go out only with married men and she answered very frankly that she likes sex but doesn't want to get involved with a man who might get serious with her. Dating a "happily" married man serves both purposes.

Another single woman, using some real twisted logic, said that the only way to avoid getting Herpes, AIDS, or VD is to date only married men, because they make love to only one woman...their wives. She didn't seem to realize that if he is cheating with her, he might be cheating with other women, too. Thus he's got just as good a chance of catching something and passing it on as do single men—maybe even more so!! Single men, with their exposure to lots of women on a daily basis, can pick and choose and be selective in their choice of dates. Married men usually have to sneak around and take whatever comes along.

Sometimes dating a married man can become habit forming. One woman (I'll call her Penny) had a casual affair (if there is such a thing) with a traveling salesman (married of course) and soon fell head over heels for the guy. She also was married at the time and had a lovely family. When his company relocated him and his family to a city thousands of miles away, she packed up too, left her family, divorced her husband and followed her lover to his new location, where they both continued their illicit affair, discreetly, right under his wife's nose. Eventually, after nearly 10 years of this double life, he divorced his wife and married Penny.

And they lived happily and suspiciously of each other ever after.

By now you readers are aware that I conduct all types of research on single people. But here is my *oddest* that you may enjoy. I asked hundreds of men and women what SIZE mate they are looking for. Here are their combined answers by age group:

	Women Want	Men Want
Ages 30-39	5'8"-6'3", 170-216 lbs.	5'6"-5'11", 106-163 lbs.
Ages 40-49	5'7"-6'2", 165-214 lbs.	5'3"-5'11", 104-143 lbs.
Ages 50-59	5'8"-6'2", 180-220 lbs.	5'2"-5'8", 113-142 lbs.
Ages 60-69	5'7"-6'0", 165-215 lbs.	5'2"-5'8", 110-139 lbs.
Ages 70 & Over	5'8"-6'1", 160-190 lbs.	5'2"-5'5", 116-144 lbs.

Just a little "trivia" for your information.

So far in this chapter, we've devoted most of the space to understanding WOMEN. Now lets pay more attention to understanding MEN.

To understand men, you have to associate with us long enough so you can find a way to dig deep down into our psyche.

I have talked with many women who thought they had met their Mr. Wonderful, only to discover too late that he wasn't anything at all like they first judged him to be. After they had associated with the man over a period of time, they discovered his real persona, and they didn't like what they saw. So, ladies don't jump to conclusions until you associate with your man over a longer period of time. My guess is that it takes a *minimum* of 6 months of closeness before you start to really know your man.

Conversely, don't jump to negative conclusions about a man either. Unless he's a real out and out slob, get to know him better before you make your final judgment. I heard from a woman who upon meeting a man for the first time stated emphatically that he wasn't her type. She was in her 40's and he was in his 50's. Her dislike for him centered more around the cosmetic than substantive reasons. She didn't like his facial features, his weak chin, and his sagging stomach. She couldn't find anything right with him, and she tended to give him the cold shoulder.

However, he continued to pursue her. One day just to get him off her case, she agreed to join him on his sailing yacht for a Sunday cruise. While they sailed on his rather large boat, he expected her to act as first mate and barked orders for her to perform certain chores with the rigging while he manned the tiller. She found herself taking directions and orders from him and thoroughly enjoying it. Before she realized it, she began to respect his ability as a leader, as a captain, and as a man who knew what he was doing. In no time, she completely forgot about his weak chin and sagging stomach and fell head over heels in love with him. And on subsequent voyages, she became a rather good first mate, too, all the while adoring her captain.

When I last heard from her, she stated that she was deeply in love with this guy, more so than she had even been with her ex-husband when they were first married. If she had stuck with her original feelings, she never would have experienced the thrill of falling in love.

Single men set up so many barriers around them that even they get confused and lost. You've got to get to know most men much better before you toss them aside as being incompatible.

Dear George:

"Men will ask me for my telephone number to call for a dinner date and then never call. Why don't they call? Is it just to make me feel they are not anxious?"

Judging from the amount of mail I get on this subject, it seems to be a big problem with single women. In my book, a man who tells you he is going to call and doesn't, after a reasonable length of time, has one of two basic problems. Either he isn't very creative and, therefore, doesn't know how to end a date with anything except a false promise, or, more likely, he figures he has you "hooked" and is now putting you on the shelf with all his other possessions. He'll probably call you someday in the distant future, when it suits his particular situation or when he can't get a date from someone else. Unless you don't mind being used as a doormat by the person, scram!

Usually men on an ego trip will give the "I'll call you soon" rubbish with no intention of following through. If you know your date is on such a trip, try this just for the fun of it (and to be a little bit nasty). When he says that he'll call you soon, tell him he needn't bother and immediately change the subject. He'll probably beg you for a chance to call you, if for no other reason than to save his bruised ego.

A man with a semblance of courtesy, who doesn't plan to go out with you on a regular basis, will usually thank you for a nice time (it's probably a lie) and wish you good luck on your job, or in your new home, or something of that nature and let it go at that. In other words, he'll be polite without giving you false hopes.

Conversely, if a man has enjoyed being with you, he'll have his own special way of letting you know it and you'll probably hear from him again real soon. The safe way is not to read anything into what he says until he follows through on it.

One last thing: If you have been getting a lot of men putting you off like this, maybe it's YOUR fault. If you are too cold or aloof on a date, the guy probably figures it will take until he's 99 years old to warm you up, and it's not worth it. Or if you are the clinging vine type, gushing all over him, the distant sound of wedding bells may scare him off. Check yourself out. And while you're at it, check out your appearance in a full-length mirror.

Finding Mr. Wonderful is a science, not an art.

Dear George:

"Why do men go to singles dances and not ask women to dance? What are they there for?"

Many men are basically shy when it comes to women. Women don't believe this, but it's true. Many men just can't get up the nerve to ask a strange woman to dance. Many can't even ask one they've known for a while because they feel they aren't good enough as far as dancing ability is concerned. I think women have attached so much importance to a man's dancing capabilities that men are intimidated unless they actually know they are great dancers.

I ran a survey among single men, asking them if they felt comfortable asking a strange woman to dance. A whopping 75 percent said they feel *uncomfortable* asking a strange woman to dance. However, all said they probably would dance with a strange woman if SHE gave the impression that she was interested in meeting them.

Most of the men I surveyed said they can't face being rejected. Others said the women make it look as though they are waiting for their dates to arrive. Almost half said they felt they weren't a good enough dancer compared to the men "she" had already danced with that evening. And half said they only dance the slow dances, and when one comes along, the woman is usually besieged with other dance partners and it's too late. It's a vicious circle.

Dear George:

"You printed a letter from a man about possessive women and his complaints on the subject. Now I want to complain about men, especially self-centered men. Do you realize how boring it is for women on a date to listen to you men telling us what YOU want, YOUR opinions, goals, ideas, ad nauseam. You men kill any chance of a relationship by being so self-centered and talking about YOU all the time."

The Bible tells us that Sampson killed 20 thousand Philistines with the jawbone of an ass. I suspect that just as many relationships have been killed with the same weapon, if you get my drift.

The problem is that self-centered people—men and women—don't realize they are this way and how boring they really are. They are talking about their favorite subject—themselves—and to them that's sheer enjoyment and excitement.

It's too bad that more people can't take the hint. When a person will only go out with you one time and no more, you should immediately check your breath, your deodorant, or your conversation.

Dear George:

"When you accept a drink from a strange man in a bar, does he expect something in return?"

You can bet your sweet bippie he does! At the least he expects some conversation in return. At the most? . . . well . . .

If a man buys you a drink and bypasses the less attractive gals in the lounge, there's perhaps a spark of romantic interest lurking in that drink, and it's aimed directly at you. It's his mating call! When you accept his drink, you usually must also plan to accept at least some chitchat from him no matter how boring it might become. I'm not saying this is all bad. I know lots of great friendships that started this way. But if you happen to get stuck with a real bore whom you can't easily shake, it makes it a mighty expensive drink for you.

If you ever find yourself in such a position in which you can't get rid of the guy, try this: Look at your wristwatch and remark, "I can't understand what's keeping my fiance. He had a late meeting at the Sheriff's department, where he works, but he should be off duty by now."

On the other hand, if this guy buys a round for everyone at the bar, that's a different story. He's probably being overly generous, celebrating some accomplishment, or showing off his wealth. If this often happens in places where you go, let me know. I've got a whole bunch of freeloading friends waiting to frequent your lounge.

Dear George:

"Why are so many of you men neurotic?"

Maybe it's because we have nothing better to do.

Dear George:

"What did I do wrong? I went with this man half a dozen times and we got along great...and I mean really great! He let me know he cared, and just as things were going really well, he abruptly stopped seeing me. He hasn't returned my calls or a note I wrote him. I hear

he tells everyone how much he likes me, but I can't get a peep out of him. What gives?"

I don't think you did anything wrong. It looks to me like you got a scared "jack rabbit" who is now hiding in his den, reveling at how lucky he was to escape capture by a "fox." Chances are he's been divorced once or twice and is very leery of getting involved again. This happens to a lot of singles. I do think he should at least have the decency to return your phone calls or drop you a note, but maybe this tells you how scared he really is. He's sort of burying his head in the sand, hoping these serious thoughts he's having will just fade away. It sounds to me like you almost landed him.

I know that most gals would say to drop him like a hot potato, but I say hold on a little longer. If you have planted a seed, you have to keep watering it if it's ever going to flower. I'd drop him a short note—not gushy or demanding—just friendly, wondering what's happening in his life. I'd write one every 3 or 4 weeks, so as not to appear pushy. If you can, try to be seen with other men at parties or functions that he or his friends might attend (the old jealousy bit). Try it for 3 months or so and see what happens. If nothing happens, then maybe the seed turned out to be a weed. It happens!

Dear George:

"How do you turn down a man who asks you to dance and then accept another man's offer minutes later, without insulting the first man?"

Life sure gets complicated, doesn't it? Let's face it! When you turn down a man, you've already insulted him somewhat. And by accepting another man's invitation a few minutes later, you add injury to insult. Normally, the first man will take the hint (and hate you for the rest of his life, probably). But to avoid hurt feelings, when you turn down a man, maybe you should say that you are just not in a dancing mood right now and thank him

for asking you. Then, when you accept another man, it could be interpreted that your "dancing mood" has changed, giving the first man a chance to salvage some of his ego.

It's refreshing to see that someone is interested in avoiding hurting another's feelings. I've seen plenty of instances in which the women couldn't care less about the man's feelings.

Dear George:

"When a lady is asked to dance and then the man proceeds to make vulgar moves on the dance floor, what is the best way to show disapproval of such behavior, other than simply walking off the floor? I am a very affectionate person and enjoy dancing very much. But the dance floor is not the place for suggestive and pawing actions. I know of no women who find this complimentary. I wonder if this type of male is only capable of performing on a dance floor. What is the male point of view?"

Probably most people—male and female—would suggest that you stuff barbed wire down his shorts. Of course, you should walk off the dance floor and ignore the jerk completely.

One "creep" can ruin it for a hundred nice guys, so be sure you don't fall into the trap of judging everyone else by the actions of one person.

And before you women become overly smug, I'm sure for every guy who is a creep, there's probably a woman who is the same (a "creepette"?). I know of plenty of instances in which the gals have been just as suggestive on the dance floor and even worse. I also know of several instances in which women have followed perfect strangers home from a lounge unbeknownst to the men, because the women "wanted to get to know them better." I guess before we condemn one gender, we should accept the fact that both sexes share the blame equally. Like the old saying goes, "What's sauce for the goose is sauce for the gander." (But who wants a sauced goose?)

Dear George:

"I've read your column for several years, and I always seem to notice that your letters from women complain about men attacking them on the dance floor, etc. Don't you ever get letters from men complaining about women? What bothers me the most is women who have too much to drink and then try to force us to dance with them. I've had them actually drag me onto the dance floor; if I didn't go along with them, I would have lost a shirt sleeve. This has happened more than once. Say something for the men for a change."

I agree with you wholeheartedly. I'm sure that every man has nearly lost an arm—or a wristwatch—trying to pull away from a tipsy lady who must dance at all costs. And if you are successful in pulling away and avoiding her, she'll be the first to spread the story that you are conceited or antisocial or some such rubbish. She usually ends up ruining the evening.

Ladies, if a man wants to dance with you, he'll ask, unless it's a ladies choice dance. If you get a bashful one and feel you have to do the asking, fine! But don't force the issue into an embarrassment for both of you. Let's face it! Like it or not, some men don't enjoy dancing.

Dear George:

"How do you handle those rejecting "nos" from men?"
That's a switch! Usually it's us men who hear the "nos!"

To avoid getting a "no" answer, why not follow the rules of good salesmanship? A good salesman never asks a question in such a way that he can get "no" for an answer. He instead usually offers a choice of something or something, instead of a choice of yes or no. Maybe you can work this into whatever it is you've been asking them.

Here are a few examples of offering a choice of something or something, rather than a choice of yes or no:

"Would you care to dance to this tune,
or would you rather wait for a slower one?"
(You give two choices that can't be answered with a no!)
"Would you care to join me for dinner on a weekday,
or is the weekend better?"
(Again, a choice of something or something)
"Your place or mine?" (How can he refuse?)

Finally, in response to an anonymous woman who—without even being asked—sent me a list of the things she doesn't like about men. She sounded like a pretty sharp gal despite her negative comments, so I thought I would devote some time to straighten out her misconceptions once and for all!

First, she doesn't like pot-bellied men. Lady, those are not "pot-bellies." The medical term for them is "Door Openers Paunch!" Men develop this paunch after decades of opening car doors and restaurant doors for you women, along with pulling out chairs and doing sundry and other chivalrous acts. You can always spot a true gentleman by the size of his "Door Openers Paunch." The bigger it is, the more of a gentleman he is. Beware of men with tight abs and pecs. They probably are not gentlemanly and probably should be avoided by discriminating women.

The next thing she doesn't like is "hair strands swept across a bald head." The answer to this one is easy! We all know that bald people possess a superior intellect to the rest of us. The balder they are, the smarter they are. That's because as their brain expands with increased knowledge, it forces the hair follicles out of the scalp and leaves no room for them to regrow. But a lot of men don't want to flaunt the fact that they are smarter than the rest of us so they try to conceal this obvious fact by either wearing a hat, a toupee, or combing whatever hair they have left over the bald spot. That is really the final valiant effort to preserve their modesty and gentlemanliness while trying to hide their obvious superiority.

Ladies, wake up! These are true gentlemen who are trying to

be modest and not showoffs! They are making a desperate effort to make you feel comfortable by not exposing their obvious intellectual superiority. These men are very considerate and should be sought after by all women for the true "catches" they really are.

Next she says she doesn't like men with ill-fitting pants. She doesn't know the facts behind this phenomenon either. These men with so-called "ill-fitting" pants at one time had all their pockets jam-packed and bulging with *cash*! But, as they spent more and more of their money on you women, their pockets emptied but there still remained a pocket sag caused by the bulging of the fabric. If these guys hadn't been so generous buying you women everything (dinners, theater, yachts, villas, cruises, etc.), their pockets would still be bulging and their pants would be tight fitting. Again, you gorgeous women are totally to blame!

Then she says she doesn't like men who dye their hair darker! (Lady, puleeese! Every *woman* in town colors her hair. Be fair!) The reason men dye their hair darker is to show their respect for you women. It makes them look younger so when they take you out in public everyone thinks you nailed some younger stud, thus helping build your own ego and public esteem. They do it just for YOU!

And her final complaint: men with whistling hearing aids! Again, the woman's fault. I researched this with 146,000 single men who use "whistling" hearing aids and they told me that when they get a pooped pucker from whistling at you gorgeous women all day long, they turn up the whistle on their hearing aid so they can give their lips a rest. Seems normal to me!

This lady had a few other negative comments about men but I think I answered the bulk of them based on the scientific evidence I was able to amass. If you female readers meet any men who fit the above descriptions, grab them and hang on for dear life. You've met your soul mate, thanks to this anonymous reader. But first, turn down his hearing aids!

Chapter Eleven

AGE AND THE AGE DIFFERENCE

This is another touchy subject . . . but I haven't shied away from touchy subjects so far, and I'm not going to start now.

Dear George:

"I am a 59 year old widower, fairly well off, and have been dating a gorgeous 32-year-old gal. I've been thinking of taking the plunge and getting married but am concerned about the age difference. What do you think?"

If she starts calling you Da-Da, you'll know she's searching for a father image, since you are old enough to be her dad. Twenty years from now, when you're a tired 79, she'll be a lively 52. How are you going to keep her mind off the hordes of younger men who will undoubtedly vie for her attention. I know of several successful marriages between people with greater age disparities than yours, but I know of a lot more that aren't successful. I guess the things to look for are how mature she is and how caring she is, and what lasting attributes YOU possess, other than your money, to keep her interest during your "golden years." Another question to ask is, "Is she in love or looking for security?" There are an awful lot of things to be considered before you plunge into marriage with this wide age difference. It might be better if you instead plunged into a cold shower!

Dear George:

"Why do men in their 50's usually prefer much younger women, instead of a compatible companion for the rest of their lives?"

Maybe it's because they don't think the women they know in

their own age groups are really compatible for the rest of their lives. Please note the following letter.

Dear George:

"(It sounded like several of your readers thought poorly of a man dating a woman 25 years younger than he. If you haven't tried it, don't knock it!) I'm 34 years old, considered quite attractive, and have been dating a man 57. He's not rich, so I'm not a gold digger. But he is caring, considerate, and thoughtful. Every time I go out with him, I learn something new, or we go to a new place. He isn't boisterous, knows his manners, can hold his liquor, and is a perfect gentleman. I'm proud to be seen with him."

Many people still feel that with the age difference between you, sooner or later you're going to stop caring for him—just about the time when he reaches the age when you must *start caring* for him, if you get my drift.

Dear George:

"How do you get a guy who is younger than you are to ask you out?"

How much younger? Five years? No sweat! Use the same feminine wiles you use to get older men to take you out. But if you are talking about a LOT younger, you'll probably first have to convince him that you both are on the same wave length and that there isn't a severe generation gap between you. Then follow up with your usual feminine wiles. When all else fails, you still have us old bucks waiting in the wings.

Dear George:

"Why won't a younger fellow date an older woman? Are they afraid of what society will think of them? I'm an older widow who is still attractive and sexy, but younger men seem scared. I'd be interested in your comments."

I asked a number of men this same question, and here is a brief recap of their comments:

> An accountant in his 30's said older women have a tendency to "talk down" to younger men. They've been around more and traveled more and don't hesitate to let the younger man know that they don't think he is up to her caliber of experience and intelligence.
>
> A 40-ish man said older women are too possessive. If you act friendly toward them, they misinterpret it and don't want to let you go. They seem to want to "own" you right away and act insulted if you don't respond in like manner.
>
> One man felt that women age quicker than men do, and a pretty 50 year old today might not look "so good" 5 years down the road. He said there's a certain amount of pride connected with dating.
>
> A yuppie computer programmer said he wouldn't go out with a woman 20 years older than he is because she'd be his mother's age, and he couldn't handle the thought. He did say, however, that he wouldn't mind a woman up to 5 years older than he, provided she was at his level in the things that interested him.

Most men are in the habit of dating younger women because, as we've been told all our lives, women mature much earlier than men. Thus, if the man is 4 or 5 years older than the woman, then they're about equal in maturity levels, so the story goes.

To this I say, BUNK!

I have met women 10 years older than I who don't have the maturity of a mayfly. And I've met many women 10 years younger who are extremely mature. I say that everyone has to be judged according to his or her individual merits, not with a broad brush stroke. The important thing is how two people relate to ne another. Are they comfortable with each other? Do they share the same feelings and ideas? Are they compatible? These are the things that make for a happy life.

Speaking personally, I have enjoyed many great times with women older than I and I didn't find any of the problems these interviewees expressed.

But I've noticed my mail in recent years has carried more and more letters from women wanting to date younger men. What's wrong with us old bucks? We can still do everything the young guys can. We just do it with more finesse . . . and more rest periods.

Dear George:

"I've been reading with interest your columns about older women dating younger men. One fellow said to me that men don't date older women because they cost too much. He's not scared; he just can't afford us. But fear not. Most of us grannies would just like a dancing partner or an escort to go places with. Most of us would be happy to go Dutch treat just to have an escort."

I once met a man at a singles party who was in his mid-70's. He had just filed for a divorce from his bride of 4 months. He told me that he had married a 49-year-old woman against the advice of nearly everyone he knew. In this case, it wasn't so much because of the 25-year age difference between the bride and groom. The main reason for the negative advice was that the woman had a 14-year-old son living with her, and a boy at that age is too much for a man in his 70's to help raise. But the man wouldn't be deterred. He loved the woman and—son or no son—the wedding went ahead as planned.

Moments after the bride and her son moved into his home, trouble started. He wanted the boy to be raised the same way he had raised his own sons half a century earlier, and he couldn't understand why his advice wasn't followed (and, in fact, was scorned).

The difficulties of coping with a young son ended this marriage before it ever got a chance to start. In this case, the "age difference" skipped a generation, and the marriage was ruined because of the vast age differences between the *man* and the *boy*.

In all my experience interviewing singles who got remarried, the biggest problems encountered in their married lives were associated with raising stepchildren. And if there is a great age disparity between the marriage partners, the problems are even worse. Also, the situation is DOUBLY hazardous if the children's natural father or mother lives nearby and sees the children often, dispensing contrary advice to that given by the new stepparent about how the children should behave. It can become a nightmare.

One problem I have seen time after time is where an *older woman* falls head over heels in love with a *younger man*, who eventually leaves her for a woman younger than himself. The older woman then becomes totally devastated. Many of these women firmed-up their bodies with a regular gym routine, had face lifts and plastic surgery to make themselves look and feel younger to no avail. I personally spoke with eight of these women. They really looked great and were in great shape and I have to commend them on their efforts. They looked *super*! But the crushing blow of being shunted aside for a younger woman sent *seven* of these women to psychiatrists couches . . . for many, many months.

I spoke with another very gorgeous lady who had been with her much younger boyfriend for 17 *years*. Seventeen years of a great relationship (she thought). They even bought a large home together and fixed it up together. For all intents and purposes, they were identical to a happily married couple . . . until, that is, the day he moved out and informed her that he had just recently married the much younger girl he had been secretly dating for the past two years. What a blow that had to be! I met her three weeks after he announced his secret marriage and she looked hollow-eyed from crying day and night, and also was very mistrustful of any man. (A big mistake to make us pay for the last guy's mistake). I hope she has since recovered and is happily on her way to a better relationship, possibly with an older stud.

How about his one? A newlywed woman I talked to continued to meet her previous (younger) boyfriend on the sly while her new husband was at work. That marriage lasted about a year.

Here's another shocker. The third marriage of this cute gal (age 44) was with a "trophy" husband (age 37). One day she caught him in the sack with the girlfriend of her son (from her first marriage). The mother threw the new husband out, the son threw his girlfriend out; and the ex-husband moved in with the much younger girlfriend. . . and it lasted about a year before she moved in with a younger new boyfriend. Sounds like a Peyton Place, doesn't it?

And another. . . This pleasant couple had been married for 25 years, had a nice home and seemed very compatible. Then the wife met a younger (married) Lothario and left her home and her faithful husband to be with this "stud", even though he told her he wouldn't leave his wife and only wanted her for his pleasures. And she went along with it! Whatever happened to self respect? It amazes me how someone could leave a secure family life (even it if may have been boring at times) to become someone else's "Toy" to be used at his convenience.

The most bizarre examples of older women chasing younger men are the cases of the school teachers who have been featured in the national media for seducing their adolescent male students. That's really carrying this "May/December" relationship too far. But it happens!

Remember a few pages back where I asked men why they WOULDN'T date older woman? Next, I asked different men why they WOULD date older women.

I asked them all "Why do you think younger men want to date older women?" Surprisingly, the majority of answers had to do with finances . . . but it's not the kind you might be thinking of. None of them were chasing after her money. They instead were just happy that she was financially set and he doesn't have to buy her lots of things she needs like cars, her dog's shots, car insurance, her rent, etc. Many said that older women are more stable and know what they want, while younger women are still "flighty" and naive and play games.

A few said older women are more experienced and seem to have fewer inhibitions than young gals. Most agreed that older women aren't gold diggers. One man responded "they pay their own way." Half said that women look and dress younger, work out in gyms and get cosmetic surgery and want to BE younger, so they seek out younger guys. Several added that "older women don't run me ragged with all kinds of sports activities." Other comments: "Younger women play childish mind games while older women know what they want." "Older women are more sociable and cooperative and save us the hassle of the pursuit." "I like women of any age." "They don't have bratty kids around."

Unfortunately, the down side of all this was the final question I posed: "If a cute woman five years your junior came onto you strong and didn't have the bad traits you mentioned, what would happen to your May/December relationship?" I think we all can guess what all of the answers were to this question, and that's probably why we have these seven devastated older women out there right now.

And finally, I asked one woman trying to get over a four-year relationship after her much younger man split the scene, why she thought women went for younger men? She said that a few years ago it was a "fad" for women to seek out younger relationships and she went for it. Now, she says, she's paying the emotional price.

Chapter Twelve

THE IMPORTANCE OF DANCING

Let's face it men! Most women would rather dance than eat. Conversely, most men would rather eat than dance. Women will more readily attend a singles *dance* than any other type of singles activity.

We already read a letter from a woman wondering why men attend a dance but don't ask women to dance. We covered that issue pretty well so that women can now understand us shy men better. But it still left a lot of unanswered questions. So guess what?

I took it upon myself to conduct a survey among thousands of women—widowed and divorced— to discover why they like to dance so much. I figured that if men knew the answer to that question, we could adjust our attitudes and, with our newfound understanding of dancing, become better dancing partners.

So I ran an exhaustive survey among the female readers of my singles column and asked them to check off over sixty items of information. I had firmly resolved that once and for all we men would understand and appreciate why women die for dancing. I also asked my married readers to respond, separately.

These results will probably reinforce women's feelings about dancing. But they were a real eye-opener for men like me. As a result of this survey, I developed a whole new outlook on dancing and am now an enjoyable dancing partner—stepping on toes aside.

Of the 6,400 replies I received, here are the four most important reasons why women said they like to dance, in order of importance:

1. Women love music and would rather share it with a man.
2. A woman likes her body moving in rhythm with a man's.

3. Women think dancing is intimate and sexy, and has sexual connotations.
4. Women feel it is romantic and part of the courting ritual.

As part of this same survey, I asked women of all ages what type of dance they liked the most. This also was a shocker. The most popular form was Latin dancing, followed by slow dancing (foxtrot, two-step, etc.), with swing (jitterbug) in third place, and disco in fourth. A close fifth place went to the waltz.

Another question I asked was what type of person women preferred to dance with. Most prefer a partner who was as tall or taller and, in second place, one who was a good dancer or liked dancing. Next came "good conversationalist" and sense of humor, followed in fourth place by "slim" or in good physical shape.

Armed with this information, I'm sure most of us men will now know how to approach the dance floor with more confidence.

Chiropodists and podiatrists. . . here we come!

Since this is an equal opportunity book, it's only fair that we discuss the male gender's attitudes toward terpsichorean activity. I'm sure some of the comments I came up with will be just as eye opening to the women as some of their comments were to us men. (And keep in mind, there are many men who LOVE to dance, God Bless them! These comments are for the rest of us.)

Dear George:

"I read your column before I do anything else. I noticed where several women had written you complaining about men who sit at a dance and don't ask women to dance. I see it all the time at every dance I attend, even at the dance parties at the studios where I take dancing lessons. What's wrong with you men? Are you afraid of us dainty little women? We're the weaker sex, aren't we?"

Weaker sex? Baloney! Anyone who can give birth to a baby and be back on her feet an hour later doesn't sound very weak to me. If men delivered babies, it would take most of us 6 months to recover, and then another 6 months to complain about it.

But as far as men not asking women to dance, I have researched this over the years by quizzing hundreds of non-dancing men. When I asked them why they don't dance, I got a lot of really solid reasons. You women, instead of fighting it, should figure out ways to overcome it.

Here are my survey results from non-dancing men:

1. **Many (if not most) men are basically shy.** I mentioned this in a previous chapter, and it bears repeating again, since it was the most prevalent reason for not dancing. Many men will NEVER ask to dance with a woman to whom they've not been introduced. I know you women refuse to believe it, but this reason tops the list.

2. **Many men lack confidence in their dancing ability.** If a man doesn't feel he is a good dancer, and he sees the dance floor crammed with Fred Astaire-types, he'll be reluctant to dance because he doesn't want to be the worst dancer on the floor.

3. **Many men simply don't like dancing.** But then, you ask, why does he even bother to go to a singles dance if he doesn't like to dance? His answer, "But where's a better place to meet single women than at a singles dance?"

4. **Many men don't like women's attitudes.** (Here we go again with that ATTITUDE word). The men figure if the woman doesn't look like she cares about dancing—or about dancing with him in particular—why bother to get turned down.

5. **Many men fear rejection.** I don't care who he is and how tough he might be, when a man asks a woman to dance and she says no, to many men this rejection is very painful. It's sort of like having a circumcision at age 50, performed by a nervous intern. So, rather than face the possibility of

being rejected, a lot of men just won't bother to ask in the first place, *unless* (and I've said this before because it's so important for women to understand) *the woman makes the first move or shows some interest in him.*

6. **He may find the available dancing partners undesirable.** Let's face it. A man doesn't dance because he wants to wear out some shoe leather. He dances because you are attractive to him in one way or another, whether it's your dancing ability, personality, magnetism, looks, figure, inheritance, money, etc. If you don't fit into one of the categories that HE finds desirable, then you are undesirable, *at least to him.* Everyone appreciates different things.

7. **He may be turned off by certain women.** Some people just turn off other people. I remember once when a woman approached me in a local nightspot. She had recognized me and started to bawl the hell out of me because none of the men in the place had asked her to dance. THIS LADY WAS A REAL TURNOFF, to me and to every guy in the place, and I could quickly understand why. First of all, she sized up all the men as if she were planning to give them a proctological examination, and this turned men off pronto. Her conversation was totally negative and complaining. And when she got close enough, it was obvious that she must have recently fallen into a vat of fresh garlic sauce, as every time she breathed, it melted the hairs in my nostrils. A real turn-off person. I must say, I was really proud of the men that evening.

Maybe these survey results will allow you women to turn a wallflower into an "Astaire." A good way to get started is to use the "ladies choice" dances that most singles gatherings offer. It's your chance to show the bashful men that you are interested in them, without being pushy. And when you finally drag your Mr. Wonderful onto the dance floor, give him some kind of pleasant compliment to put him at ease. He might just want to come back for more—and then you're "off and running." But be honest in your compliment. Don't tell him how light he is on his feet after he has just imprinted "Cats Paw" all over your white shoes. A little honest compliment or reassurance on your part will go a long way toward making him feel comfortable with you. "Ladies choice" dances were invented for one reason—they work!

Why don't you women make a concerted effort at the next singles dance you attend to identify the types of men listed here, and see what you can do to change them. It should be fun.

Now let me repeat a few words of caution. I've already mentioned it but it is important to emphasize it again: If you decide you want to be a great dancer and learn all the latest steps, whether you are male or female, beware of dance studio scams. Don't sign any contract unless you know exactly what you are signing and you have checked on the credulity of the dance studio (BBB, Attorney General, etc.). Here's one reason why! *Smooth* dancing instructors in a large Florida city signed-up an 80 year old man for $100,000 worth of dance lessons. I think he'd have to live to be 150 years old (and still be able to stand) to get his money's worth from this scam. Luckily the state's attorney intervened and got most of his money back.

As I stated previously, a word to the wise is sufficient.

Chapter Thirteen

WIDOW'S PITFALLS

Readers might wonder "why does he devote" a chapter to widow's pitfalls when we've already read about dozens of pitfalls. It's because of the wide variety of pitfalls there are and the importance of recognizing one when we encounter it. As with any course we chart in life, there are many different potholes and detours that must be encountered and bypassed as we journey to our destination. Some pitfalls of single life may be stranger than those of married life. But once we identify them for what they are, we can easily learn to cope with them or ignore them. Pitfalls in single life are really no big deal if we don't make them such.

Dear George:

"Do you have a sure-shot rebuke or answer to a married man making a proposition to you because you are a widow?"

That's easy! Take your choice. Tell him one of the following:

1. **"I'm an old friend of your wife."**
2. **"My new boyfriend is an insanely jealous rifle-marksman."**
3. **"I'll call you when my herpes subsides."**
4. **"It's okay as long as you bring a letter from your wife."**
5. **"Bug off you creep!"**

I prefer number 5!

Dear George:

"I am a widow and take care of my 82-year-old mother. She

doesn't want me to date anyone or go anywhere at all. She resents it. Any answers will help."

I am assuming your mother has her full mental faculties. If so, then my next question is: Who is going to care for you when YOU'RE 82? Judging from the rest of your letter, you've been a very dutiful daughter, and your mother should bless the day she bore you. And she should expect you to live your own life as much as possible. By all means, go out on as many dates as you can. Lord knows good dates are hard enough to find as it is, and if you get a good one, grab him!

Perhaps you can get a neighbor to check on your mother while you're out. And if you are gone for an extended stay, you can usually hire someone to keep an eye on her. You can also install a security system that monitors her well-being. I think most people would say it's best to explain to your mom that you also have a life to live, then go live it. Here's another idea: Why not find an 82-year-old man for her and double date? She might even teach you a thing or two.

Dear George:

"Since you've run so many singles dances and parties, maybe you can tell us first-time women what kind of men to be wary of."

I've touched on it before, but I'm glad to do it again. On a very few occasions, you'll find con men or just plan "weirdos" stalking a singles get-together, looking for some gullible women who will become their next victims. It could be an investment broker, a sex fiend, or a host of other unsavory types for the perfect "target." No one said the singles scene is perfect, nor is the married scene, for that matter.

Here are a few ways to help avoid being victimized by unsavory men at a singles party:

Don't be misled because the guy is handsome,

well dressed, or a smooth talker. The best con men in the world are all these and more. Pay attention to what's underneath the facade.

Leave your diamonds and jewelry at home. They'll only attract the unattractive.

Don't be snowed because he's a good dancer. Pay attention to everything else about him. And follow the advice I gave earlier in this book about not giving out telephone numbers and addresses until you KNOW it's okay.

One time when I had published this advice in one of my newspaper columns, a widowed reader evidently forgot about it and soon thereafter met a man who she thought was the answer to a widow's prayers. They went dancing almost every night (he was such a marvelous dancer—so light on his feet, she said). He was handsome, polite, slim, and trim, and very well dressed. She showed him off every chance she could to other single ladies, who were not as fortunate as she. She was totally snowed by the guy and never even bothered to check into his background. You know the rest of the story.

They got married. She bought him a new home. She added his name to her sizable checking and savings accounts, and gave him power of attorney over her securities. She was in love, blindly.

But the love lasted only until she discovered that he was a philanderer, not to mention a heavy drinker. These things were pretty well known to just about everyone else in town, but she went into the relationship with both eyes shut! After all, he was such a marvelous dancer. . . and so polite!

To make a long story short, she lost just about everything she had. She even lost the respect of her single women friends, who were not as "fortunate" as she.

That's why you'll find me repeating myself when it comes to cautioning women not to rush blindly into an affair until they

REALLY know the guy. The waters of single life are teeming with all kinds of piranhas, sharks and other predators.

A big pitfall for women is all the married men who think that single women are easy prey because they are alone—and lonely—and not having enough sex on a regular basis. These men "charitably" offer their "services" (whenever their wives aren't around). For some attractive widows this can be a major problem. So here is one of my columns that I addressed to married women. ("Surprisingly, a large portion of the mail I receive is from married people).

Attention Married Women!

Do you know where your husbands are? It seems lately that we must be having a testosterone explosion because I suddenly see way too many married men trying to pick up single women. Naturally, they all remove their wedding rings first, and the single women usually don't know they're married. We single men have enough competition for all the gorgeous ladies. We don't need any more.

I asked a few of these jerks why they weren't wearing their wedding rings, and you should have heard the wild answers, some of which were: "I live in a high crime area." "I don't want to catch it on machinery" (he works in an office), "I'm afraid I'll lose it," Etc., etc.

So married women, I have the perfect solution for you: *Tattoo* a wedding band on his wedding ring finger! Let him try to take THAT off! Then all the single gals would be able to recognize these philanderers either by his tattooed wedding ring, or by the glove he's wearing on his left hand to hide it. You can get the tattoo done in gold color for about 50 bucks. Might be the best money you've ever spent.

I can just picture the wedding of the future: the bride and groom are followed down the aisle by the ring bearer and a tattoo artist.

(There go all my married male readers.)

While we're touching on the subject of marriage, did you ever contemplate on the fact that Adam and Eve had an ideal marriage? He didn't have to hear about all the men she could have married, and she didn't have to hear about the way his mother cooked.

* * *

Here's a little amusing anecdote to close out this chapter. It's about a date from Hell! A lady wrote me about a blind date she had with a veterinarian. "He brought a dog along on our date. At first I was upset, but then I changed my mind. The dog had lots of charm. He had none."

Chapter Fourteen

SO YOU THINK YOU FOUND MR. (OR MRS.) "RIGHT" AGAIN! NOW WHAT?

"Eat, Drink and Remarry"

Are you ready to entertain some thoughts about tying the knot again? If you follow the *good* experiences of all the people I have featured in this book, it should be a done deal.

All my numerous research projects have proven that the *main reason* for re-marriage failures is that people *don't know enough about the person they marry*. Another reason is people think they can change their partner after the wedding. A big mistake!

How about this tale of not knowing enough about one's partner? (As incredible as this story seems, I checked it out personally. It's True!) The bride and groom, in all of the wedding finery, stood before the minister in the packed church as he performed the ceremony. To the groom; "do you take this woman etc., etc?" and he answered "I do". To the bride; "do you take this man etc., etc?", she answered: "Just a minute, Reverend!" Then she turned to the wondering congregation and said: "I'd like to thank my in-laws for the wonderful rehearsal dinner last evening. And, I'd like to thank my parents for the lovely wedding they planned for me. And I want to thank my maid of honor for sleeping with my fiancé last night." And with that, she stepped down from the altar, strolled through the stunned congregation, out the back door, into the limousine and went home. End of marriage before it ever started.

How's that for a shocker? She didn't really KNOW the person she had planned to marry...until the very last minute! And she didn't like what she saw. Good for her! She wasn't about to go through the ceremony and then try to change him later. She bailed out at the last minute . . . but I'm sure she had a lot of misgivings as she donned her dress and veil that morning. A real gutsy lady.

I hate to tell you how many times I have heard about newlywed husbands who tried to cheat on their wives ON THEIR HONEYMOON! It is vitally important . . . (repeat) *vitally important!*...that you must know EVERYTHING about your partner before you commit yourself. It might take a little longer, but this old saying is more important than ever in building a relationship: "Act in haste; repent at leisure!"

If you are a widower, 3 out of 4 widowers remarry within 5 years . . . and they make mistakes I just featured: Not knowing enough about their mates or thinking they can change them.

Another GIANT reason that relationships break-up is INFIDELITY! In my book *"MARRIED AGAIN: Making the Right Decision the Next Time"*, my research among 3,200 divorced persons showed 40% of the men admitted cheating in their marriage. But so did 36% of the women. It's an equal-opportunity thing!

Here's another tidbit that adds to the instability of today's marriages. On the eves of their wedding days, 65% of brides were more concerned about their dresses than whether or not they were doing the right thing.

Are you becoming tired of all my research results? Well, hold on! I only have a few more such as this one: reasons why people got married! You'll never get these statistics in any other book, so count your blessings that you only had to purchase ONE book to know *everything!*

Reasons why people got married for the *first* time: Love (60%), Lust (15%). The remainder was split-up among: Too young to know better; wanted to get away from parents; move to a big city; too late to call-off the wedding; proud of their spouses financial possibilities!

Reasons why people got married the *second* time: Love (43%). The remaining reasons were: needing financial support; needing help in raising children from previous marriage; loneliness.

Unless you do your homework, getting married or remarried is a real *gamble*. There are 75 wedding chapels in Las Vegas, with over 100,000 weddings performed every year. Maybe that's why it's called the *gambling* capitol of the world.

Keeping Your Eyes Wide Open!

Before you select a partner—a serious long term relationship partner—you both must have these ingredients baked into your partnership: LOVE . . . unabashed love for each other with no strings attached. COMMUNICATION . . . the best way to avoid boredom. (Not this: "I don't want to talk about it! I'm too tired to talk now!" One or the other monopolizes the conversation.) GENEROSITY. . . is your partner a sharing, giving person WITHOUT KEEPING SCORE? CARING...Does your partner care about you now, and will he/she care for you if you become incapacitated for any reason?

What about MENTAL ABUSE? If your partner picks apart everything you do now, how in the world could you handle that on a full-time basis? And what's your partner's record on PHYSICAL abuse? In case you didn't know it, physical abuse is our country's *number one* crime with physical abuse occurring *every 3 seconds!* It's not just men that abuse their partners. Remember Lorena Bobbit? According to all newspaper reports, she cut off her cheating husband's penis and threw it by the side of the highway. The police found it and it was subsequently surgically reattached. A comedian once commented that his 4,000 pound vehicle had been missing for 6 months and the cops couldn't find IT, but they could find Bobbit's little penis in a few hours.

But getting back to the topic at hand, be sure your partner isn't guilty of JEALOUSY or POSSESSIVENESS. We've covered these subjects pretty well—but they are important enough to reiterate!

One last thing . . . RESPECTABILITY. Remember, I mentioned a wife left her husband of 25 years for a married man much younger. He didn't want to get serious with her, he just wanted to stay with his wife and use her as his sex toy whenever he felt like it . . . and she went along with the idea. She threw away everything to be "used" by this philanderer! SICK! No Respectability!

And lastly, most important is COMPATIBILITY! Are you both compatible in your thinking, your likes and dislikes, your backgrounds? I knew a newlywed couple that were poles apart in their thinking and mannerisms. She was a well-educated assistant to a corporate treasurer and he was a truck mechanic without a high school diploma. Every Friday night as was his custom, he would cash his paycheck and go out drinking with the boys. She on the other hand would invest some of her ample paycheck for a future down payment on a home. He wouldn't change his ways. She couldn't change hers. Clash! Arguments! INCOMPATIBILITY! This marriage ended just short of its second anniversary.

What about FINANCES? Discuss these thoroughly. Is one partner bringing a mountain of debt to the marriage? One bride was an obsessive compulsive shopper and had accumulated nearly $50,000 in credit card debts. Later when the groom discovered that he was now responsible for her horrendous interest payments that he could ill afford, it placed a severe strain on the fledgling marriage. This is also an example of where a pre-nuptial agreement separating debts before and after marriage could have helped somewhat. But how do you ask your partner for a pre-nup agreement without making it sound like you don't believe your marriage will last? It's a touchy subject and that's why many people will have their attorney bring up the subject to the partner, making it appear more as a *legal* necessity for tax purposes or some such subterfuge. Women over age 55 are more likely to want a pre-nup than any other demographic. She's usually trying to protect her children's inheritance or keep a family business intact, or protect herself from his past and future debts. My research showed how pre-nups became more prevalent as the number of marriages pile up. First marriages, only 1% signed a pre-nup. Second marriages, 8% had a pre-nup. Third marriages, 25% signed a pre-nup. It might be a touchy subject, both partners should discuss it.

Chapter Fifteen

MISCELLANEOUS

How many books have you read in your life in which a chapter is entitled "Miscellaneous"? Probably none!

Well you have now! I didn't know where to put these last items. But I thought they were interesting or amusing enough to be included in this book—hence, miscellaneous.

Here are several items that deal with some *very bad timing* on the part of two women. One woman I heard from had become bored with her marriage—and her husband—after 23 years of marriage and decided to spring the surprise on him that she was in the process of filing for a divorce. Not knowing she had these feelings, he was totally shocked and angered. He immediately changed his last will and testament, and excluded her from all the things he originally had accorded her. Three weeks later, he died of a heart attack! She was left with virtually nothing!

Another woman, I'll call her Darlene, was sick and tired of her husband constantly tinkering in his workshop in the evenings. He worked all day in the world of high-tech computer manufacturing, and when he got home at night, he'd invariably head for his well-equipped workstation to tinker with new ideas and processes that continually poured from his creative mind.

Finally, her friends and neighbors convinced her that she was missing out on the fun things of life by putting up with this tinkerer, and she divorced him for incompatibility. One year to the day after the divorce, he invented a device that he patented and sold for MILLIONS OF DOLLARS! He doesn't tinker in the evenings anymore. He's too busy wining and dining gorgeous women on his new yacht!

For you married women reading this book (shame on you!) consider your "timing" before you take any drastic measures. A bird in the hand is worth two in the bush! (Also, a bird in the hand can result in a very messy hand.)

Sometimes women have to trust their husband's judgment (but only sometimes.) This husband I'm referring to here (true story) learned that he had an incurable cancer and only had several months to live. So, he told his wife he wanted a divorce and she wouldn't agree to it. He couldn't tell her that he wanted to spare her the years it would take to pay off his forthcoming medical bills; because that would have made her compliant in a conspiracy against Medicaid that could have resulted in dire consequences for her. He kept his reasoning a secret and continued to bait her with "I'm having an affair with the Doctor's nurse" and other such taunts to get her to agree to a quickie divorce. She refused to budge. NO divorce!

I met her at a party exactly seven years after her husband died and she joyfully exclaimed that she had finally paid the last of his medical bills. Seven years of scrimping and doing without. She still felt that her husband was a bad guy until I saw through the subterfuge and informed her that her husband was really a hero. He was trying to save her the burden of his medical costs, without implicating her in a felony plot. If she had had an open mind, she would have realized that in his weakened condition, he couldn't have had an affair with anyone. Now, too late, she realized that this husband she had reviled for seven-plus years was really a thoughtful, caring, loyal husband. The look on her face spoke volumes!

———————— · ————————

Let's throw in a few figures to give a little variety to this chapter.

* 46% of women would rather shop than have sex. 50% would rather eat chocolates.

* There are nearly 4 million weddings every year in the U.S. Most don't make it to 8 years. Half end by the 4th year.
* Of all these weddings, 1,250,000 involve couples—one of whom has been married before (includes widows and widowers)

The average wedding costs $22,000. Nearly 60% of all newlyweds pay their own wedding costs. They start off married life with a major financial burden (charging the reception to credit cards). This puts a big strain on their marriage from the start, often resulting in divorce. Now they are paying off TWO bills at the same time: their old wedding reception bills and their new divorce lawyers' fees. It pays to pay attention to the experiences and ideas in this book.

Here's another anecdote that proves *men are interested in maintaining good health.* This article appeared in the very prestigious New England Journal of Medicine. (Honest! It really did!)

> The New England Journal of Medicine reports that "staring at women's breasts is good for men's health and makes them live longer. A ten minute ogle at women's breasts is as good as 30 minutes in the gym. It gets the heart pumping, improves blood circulation. Gazing at women's breasts makes men healthier, cuts the risk of stroke and heart attack, and can extend his life 4 or 5 years."

Now you ladies can't criticize a man for wanting to live an extra 4-5 years can you? It might also help solve the unbalance of too many women/too few men if the guys live longer. Women will have more dates, more dancing partners, more dining and theater partners. So the next time you notice a man "staring", I think it would be polite if you would say "thank you!"

Finally . . .

I have often been asked what I get out of running singles events or encouraging widows to get out among themselves and enjoy life. I guess what I get out of it can best be answered by a letter I received from a wonderful woman who had just wedded a great man she met at one of the many singles parties I had promoted (in a lounge, naturally). I had sent the couple a wedding gift, as I do for scores of couples who meet and marry as a result of my urging and invite me to their wedding. She wrote this:

Dear George:

"The silver cake plate was beautiful. But you really shouldn't have sent us a gift. After all, you gave us each other. Your presence at the wedding was greatly appreciated because you were the man responsible for bringing us together. Thank you so much, George, for being such a wonderful person. I hope you are rewarded for all you do for other singles by finding someone really special for yourself."

I have received many, many letters similar to this one from happy people who met as a result of my urgings (or is it harangues?) in my newspaper column. Many of these people previously had been "dead in the water." In other words, their lives had become stagnant. But as a result of my bugging them to death, they have discovered that they are attractive, desirable people. They've gotten out and joined the rest of the world. It's especially necessary for widows.

I hope this book accomplishes these same results for you, the reader. No matter who you are, how you look, what size or shape you are, your age range . . . there is someone out there searching for YOU. And I suspect that person will be the perfect mate with whom you can enjoy the rest of your life.

Make it easy for you and your perfect mate to meet by being there when he or she arrives. You never know when or where it will happen, so be persistent. And above all, be happy! Be positive!

About The Author

George Blake is a successful advertising executive who suddenly became single after 18 years of marriage. He soon realized how very difficult it was to meet new single acquaintances, so he embarked on a 20 year research program among singles to determine the best ways and the best places to meet other singles. His research involved interviews with over 29,000 singles from all around the country.

He has written a popular syndicated "singles" column for 14 years which helped considerably with his research.

He also founded National Singles Week the 3rd week in September, National Widows Week the last week in June, and "Single Mothers Day" the day before National Mother's Day in May.

His book 'SINGLE AGAIN" has been revised numerous times to keep up with the changing singles scene. It is the longest selling "singles" book on the market, now in its 4th revision.

www.ingramcontent.com/pod-product-compliance
Lightning Source LLC
Chambersburg PA
CBHW071159050326
40689CB00011B/2180